Parenting Teens with Anxiety

Helping and Guiding your Teen to Improve
Mental Health and Reduce Anxiety and Stress

By

Mary C. Norris

Table of contents

About the Author

Mary C. Norris is a clinical psychologist with a deep understanding of human behaviour, and mental illnesses.

She has spent more than 8 years in the field helping tons of teenagers suffering from anxiety, depression, chronic stress, emotional dysregulation, and much more. She also has years-long experience as the parent of a child with severe anxiety. She understands the helplessness of parenting a teen with anxiety and hopes to help parents like these on a broader scale with her professional expertise.

"Parenting Teens with Anxiety" and "Self-regulation for Kids" are two of her famous marvels on parenting kids with troubled psychology and behaviour.

Preface

Anxiety is the fear, apprehension, or dread of something awful happening or of being unable to cope with a situation. Anxiety usually provokes bodily reactions such as 'butterflies in the stomach,' stress, shakiness, nausea, and sweatiness. Ultimately, it affects human behaviour such as avoiding the source of anxiety, developing unhealthy coping mechanisms, or changing their style of attachment.

Anxiety is a complex emotion with complex triggers, finding its victims mostly in the preteen and adolescent years.

Teenage is a period of emotional, physical, and social transformation that occurs simultaneously as teenage brains change. Teenagers want to try new things and want more independence. Teenagers find themselves in a constant state of concern about these transitions, opportunities, and challenges.

Feeling anxious, confused, worried, and even scared is normal and sometimes helps us reach our personal and professional goals, but matters get out of hand when these feelings make a home in you. They act as a slow poison to a human's body and brain, affecting every bit of life in you if left unbothered.

Your teenager needs your helping hand in this time, as much as scary and frustrating it may feel. I am here with a book full of practical strategies to be your trusted partner in this journey.

I understand what you are feeling. It took me years to help my teenager manage his crippling anxiety. You and your teenager can make it to the other side of the tunnel. Let's begin.

Introduction

According to a study, one-quarter of all teenagers will experience any anxiety disorder at some point in their lives. That is three hundred million teenagers.

Moreover, this number has only been gradually increasing over the years.

It is also challenging, exhausting, heart-breaking, and isolating to have a child with an anxiety problem. I have heartbreaking stories of countless teens who have come to seek my professional help on the matter.

Let's enter into the world of one of those teenagers.

Allison twisted over and kicked the sheets off her bed, unable to sleep. The time was 2:00 a.m. She could not resist checking her phone despite her commitment not to use it after bedtime. Allison had been attempting to shut down her thoughts for months. She struggled with a lot of negative self-talk, pessimism, low self-esteem, and anxiety. Allison was fatigued and tense all the time.

Life had been quite happy and stable until her father died when she was 11 years old, and her mother plunged into severe depression. Allison felt even more distant and lonely after her older brother left for college. It seemed as though her family life had come to an end. Allison did not have anyone. Allison was no longer 11 years old when her mother sought therapy for herself and began to feel better. She was sixteen and did not need or want to spend time with her mother.

Allison was distraught and blamed herself after multiple fallouts from friends. Allison's anxiousness increased as her thoughts got more negative and persistent. She began missing school due to headaches and stomach problems. It felt as if the world was falling around her. She would have frequent panic attacks. This was when she completely fell out of the radar of her social life. Things began to worsen, and she took a deep plunge into depression.

Anxiety is linked to our instinct for survival. It is a fear response (like fight or flight) when there is no real danger or threat, similar to a false alarm in your body. When emotional pain of anxiety is internalized, it emerges as depression and a loss of self-esteem. When angst is externalized, it manifests as rage-filled tantrums.

But wait, what does anxiety really feel like?

"I considered describing anxiety as a fog that obscured my thinking, but an explosion in the brain felt more fitting.

Anxiety can slam into my brain with such power that it shatters my thoughts into shrapnel that scatters in all directions. The only thing that remains is a void, a crater of emptiness.

Have you ever interacted with someone who appeared to be having an anxiety attack and noticed a blank expression on their face or a general lack of responsiveness? I am willing to bet they would love to respond to your question properly, but right now, their intellect is a crater with nothing to offer.

Thoughts sometimes feel so far away that I avoid social situations completely to avoid having to interact with the numb brain. This irritates me quite a bit at times. But the more I fight it, the more my thoughts become frozen.

So, how can I get myself unfrozen? Unfortunately, there is no simple solution. It takes time, patience, and giving myself room to unwind and contemplate in order to regain control of my mind and body."

As a parent, there is no feeling more helpless than watching your child suffer from anxiety and not knowing what to do, especially when their own brain causes the agony. Protecting your children is one of your responsibilities as a parent. But how do you deal with an invisible monster that lives within them?

I have put together this book to help you empower your teens not to lose their personality to the bully in their head. First, you will be provided with a thorough understanding of the psychology of anxiety and how it shows its face in different aspects of your teen's life. Then strategies to cope with anxiety and stress will be discussed in detail with worksheets to maximize the benefit to you and your teens.

The first chapter will cover psychology, its signs, reasons, and effects of anxiety, along with its portrayal in your teens. We will also point out the dos and don'ts of parenting teens with anxiety. The next chapter covers general guidelines to parent a teen with anxiety in the right way and how much the right parenting matters when it comes to their children's mental health. Moving on, the next five chapters cater to the five prominent ways a teen's personality is affected by anxiety and what strategies are there to deal with them. The book will be packed with case studies, research findings, and worksheets to deepen your understanding of the topic.

Teenagers are humorous and funny, and their vibrant personalities are entertaining to watch and experience; nevertheless, they may also be moody, rebellious, and anxious. Teenage years can be challenging since these young minds are caught in the limbo of creating their own identity while living under their parents' rules. During this crucial life period, teenagers are vulnerable to peer pressure and anxiety, and you, as a parent, can have a huge impact on how your teens manage their anxiety.

When it comes to parenting an anxious adolescent, the natural instinct is to anticipate challenging circumstances and strive to make them more comfortable. Parents want to have control over their children's outcomes in order to keep them comfortable, safe, and happy. All of this is motivated by love, yet it prevents kids from developing into resilient and self-sufficient people. The natural impulse is to make it better by making it go away. Still, it is the responsibility of parents to lead their kids and assist them in "figuring it out" while they are still in the secure environment of the home.

In addition to my personal knowledge of anxiety, I have 8 years of experience as a clinical psychologist. I have worked with hundreds of parents struggling to dig their teens out of the anxiety hole. I have always thought that I am lucky to have professional knowledge on the subject as I can help my own child in the best way possible. Dealing with struggling parents on a daily basis reminds me of that privilege. I wanted to help parents on a broader scale, which is the inspiration behind this book.

The strategies I have compiled in this book are well-advised to all my clients in my professional practice, and they have shown prominent improvement in their teen's anxiety.

If you are a teen exploring this book, I want you to know I understand what you are going through, and I want to help you. I assure you I will empower you to get your life back and leave the crippling anxiety behind. I have helped tons of parents and teens fight the devil of anxiety.

Now it is your turn. Let's begin.

Chapter 1: Do I Understand my Teen's Anxiety?

Anxiety affects everyone in one way or the other. It is a natural reaction to anything frightening, such as speaking in front of a group or taking a significant test. People do not always realize how severe living in a constant state of fear maybe since such sentiments are fleeting and tied to a specific cause.

Can you remember how it feels to be on the highest point of a rollercoaster? Remember the strong wave of anxiety that hits you just as you are about to fall off the edge. It is a stomach-churning sensation that lasts only a few seconds, but it can last for days or even weeks in those with chronic anxiety.

Everyone can feel anxious every once in a while during activities like public speaking or a job interview, or starting a new career or school. Anxiety is the body's emotional reaction to stress, and it can emerge as fear or anxiety about the future. While it is normal to feel anxious on occasion, persistent or repeated anxiety symptoms may suggest the presence of an anxiety disorder. Clinical anxiety can manifest itself in a variety of ways for those billions, ranging from continuous fretfulness, distractedness, and a sort of whole-body clenching to the paralyzed catastrophe of a full-blown panic attack. Everything feels bad, and you are always trying to get out of it, which usually makes things worse. But, thankfully, it is all diagnosable, manageable, and treatable.

But anxiety often leads to depression if it is left untreated. Depression may feel like a persistent sense of dissatisfaction, emptiness, and hopelessness that becomes a part of daily life. There is no joy in life. Concentration and focus are significantly more difficult to maintain, making any type of decision-making difficult. Depression can also be physically painful at times. Does it sound familiar?

"Depression feels like a burden on my shoulders, dragging me down wherever I go."

"Depression is lying behind a constructed mask, smiling while others laugh, and wishing I could just vanish."

"Depression prevents me from cleaning my hair or brushing my teeth because I am unable to move."

Your teen is not alone. Your teen is not weak. Even the most successful and famous people find anxiety crippling their lives, but they have still made the greatest contributions to our world. This gives hope that being anxiety-ridden does not mean a lost war. Oprah Winfrey, Adele, and Joey Votto are among the many celebrities to have anxiety. Some people even believe that Abraham Lincoln struggled with severe anxiety and depression. So what can stop your teens from achieving the great?

1.1 Teen Anxiety Accounts

I want to give you deep insight into what your teen's anxiety may feel for him so you and your teen can better relate to the rest of the book. I want you to know you are not alone and you can overcome this. Here's the anxiety through the lens of teens that have had close encounters with it.

Axel's Story

My teenage anxiety began when my father was diagnosed with lung cancer in November of 2016. I just recall a jumble of events: eating in a restaurant, receiving a message from my father informing me that he had gone for tests, and receiving the results the next day. I really had no idea that there was anything wrong with my father's health, so everything came as a complete surprise to me. As I walked outdoors for some fresh air, I began to have a strange sensation inside of me. I had my first panic episode at that point as I stood leaning against a wall, trying to process everything that was going on.

My anxiousness worsened as he progressed through his cancer treatment. I began to have more frequent panic attacks, and I began to avoid social situations that I used to enjoy as opportunities to socialize with my friends. But I was still certain that whatever this "teenage anxiety" thing was, I could handle it on my own, that I did not need anyone's help. I was mistaken.

My father lost his battle with cancer in May of 2017, only a year after being diagnosed with cancer. My mental health began to crumble rapidly after that. Not only were my constant emotions of anxiousness debilitating, but I also started to suffer from depersonalization, insomnia, and melancholy. I began to believe that my father's death was beginning to take its toll on me. It was obviously destroying my spirit, at the very least.

I suffered the biggest panic attack I ever had on one particular day. It became so awful that I decided to seek assistance. I knew I needed professional treatment from a therapist, and it took me a long time to get to her door, but it was ultimately what brought me back to life. Today, I work with a fantastic therapist and am looking forward to continuing on my path to recovery. I have learned to control my panic episodes and emotions, which has helped me overcome my depression, completing the healing circle.

Max's Story

When I was in high school, my father died. I spent the rest of my time there worrying if I would be able to live up to his expectations. It was a ridiculous concept, but there were moments when it was all I could think about. The way I saw the world was devastating. I could not shake the sensation that nothing I was doing was good enough, that I would never measure up to his expectations. There were weeks when it kept me awake all night, pleading for an answer that I never received. It began to improve when I sought professional assistance. I accepted the possibility that I would fall short of his expectations, but that was fine as long as I was happy with my achievements.

Heather's Story

I have had severe anxiety for as long as I can remember. In primary school, I did well intellectually, but I was socially and emotionally behind my contemporaries from the start. Middle school was my life's first major adjustment. It was quite difficult for me, but it did not appear to be so difficult for others. I despised going to school. So, I started visiting the nurse a lot to get out of class, and because I was at home, I started feeling sick a lot. My mother first saw a therapist a year after graduating from junior high and was diagnosed with generalized anxiety disorder.

When I was new in middle school, I went to the nurse's office once a week and skipped several days of school each month. Even outside of school, I was terrified. I began taking dancing classes, but I either skipped them or made excuses to stay at home. I liked dancing, but I did not want others to watch me dance. I soon began to experience low self-esteem, and became depressed. I lost my appetite, and the anorexia nervosa idea began to take shape. My teacher yelled at me, accusing me of being a slacker, and my friend judged me. I was forlorn and helpless. That summer, I began to hurt myself. My sleeping and eating habits were at an all-time low.

Finally, I went for my first outpatient anxiolytic treatment, which included cognitive behavioral therapy, and it was quite beneficial to me. Listening to music, calling friends, talking to myself, reading, writing, and chewing candy was among the coping skills I learned.

It was the best year I had had in a long time, and I only missed five days of school. I am on medications that seem to function in wonderful ways for me. I also see a therapist and keep my parents and friends in my current situation. I am in a good place and feel much better than I did many years ago.

Bryan's Story

I was a straight-A student with a lot of extracurricular activities who struggled with anxiety. My professors, with whom I had a close relationship at the time, were initially unaware of the issue because my anxiety only resulted in good marks. The dam, however, eventually burst. My grades fell, and I began to consider suicide. I ultimately went to my primary care physician, who told me it was anxiety-related, so I took a second opinion from a neurologist, who told me the same thing. I was first resistant to the diagnosis, telling a friend that I wished the doctor had told me I had brain cancer instead. I found neurosurgery to be more acceptable than therapy and drugs.

Despite these setbacks, I remain optimistic about the future. I am now living at home and not attending school. I would have sought care sooner if I had known more about my problem years ago and not considered it a taboo.

I hope these stories give you hope and help you in your journey.

1.2 Anxiety Magnets for Teens

Anxiety often hums along in the background of a normal teenager's life, given the variety of changes and uncertainties he or she faces. Anxiety can become a chronic, high-pitched state for certain kids, interfering with their ability to attend school and perform to their academic potential. It becomes difficult to participate in extracurricular activities, to make and keep friends, and maintain a supportive, flexible connection within the family. Anxiety can sometimes be limited to vague, free-floating feelings of unease. Other times, it manifests itself as panic episodes and phobias.

Why are teens prone to anxiety and stress?

Changing Brain Structure

The brain experiences significant neuronal growth and restructuring during adolescence, resulting in alterations in connection within and across distinct brain regions. This change is filled with potential booby traps and minefields for most teenagers.

According to some research, human brain growth and connectivity do not reach full maturity until around 25. 'The rental car companies claim the right thing," according to some researchers. The brain is not entirely mature at age 16 when a teenager can acquire a driver's license; or at age18, when they can vote; or at age 21, when most of them can drink, but it is closer to being mature at age 25 when they can rent a car.

The brain connectivity, its structure and behavior of teenagers are all interwoven. While young adults develop new levels of emotional regulation and complex thinking, their brains undergo changes directly required to sustain these abilities.

Researchers have discovered a gene called DCC that may be responsible for healthy brain connectivity during teenage. Small changes in DCC throughout adolescence can lead to major changes in prefrontal brain function in life later on.

During adolescence, DCC is related to the dopamine network in the prefrontal brain. The researchers discovered that the malfunction of this gene during teenage has behavioral repercussions that can last in adulthood using mouse models. Teens are particularly prone to psychiatric problems, such as depression, schizophrenia, and drug addiction, at this stage of brain development.

Researchers studied DCC expression in brains of the patients who had committed suicide to see if the findings of such basic research might be applied to human subjects. According to the study, teens who committed suicide had levels of DCC gene 48 percent more than control subjects.

Ineffective Parenting Style and Influence

While you never want to be accused of neglecting or under parenting your children, you also do not want to be accused of over parenting.

What do I really mean by that? Protecting your children constantly will impair their ability to deal with unpleasant, anxiety-inducing events. Failure to manage difficult situations effectively can lead to anxiety disorders in the future.

In some circumstances, the inverse can occur. Your teens may be so used to being shielded and numb to certain situations that doing the reverse of what their parents preach makes them feel more independent. Parents who overprotect their teens from drugs and alcohol, for example, may cause their children to become too interested, which may lead to substance abuse.

Meanwhile, judgmental, dismissive parenting can lower a child's self-esteem and cause anxiety or despair. The same thing can be said for judging your children's self-worth or body image. Children already have a lot of emotions to deal with, and rigidity might hinder their development.

Moreover, like many illnesses and diseases, mental health disorders tend to run in families and can be passed on from parent to kid. The American Journal of Psychiatry put forward research that tracked children of depressed parents for 20 years to see how they managed as adults. They discovered that children whose parents were depressed were three times more likely to develop mental health and substance misuse problems than children whose parents were not depressed.

It is vital to understand that just because a parent has a mental health problem does not guarantee it will affect their children. Itis instead about how a parent's mental health influences their behavior.

Struggling in a Changing Body

Puberty is a chaotic time when emotions, looks, and internal chemistry change at a breakneck speed. As a result, it is no surprise that this phase of development is also a time of high tension, which may sometimes lead to the all-too-common teenage angst, as well as panic and suicidal thoughts.

Estrogen, a female sex hormone, has been associated with depression for a long time. Girls' estrogen levels rise considerably during puberty, possibly contributing to the rise in depression rates.

Moreover, the age at which puberty begins may influence the depression rate. Children who are "early" or "late developers" are more likely to experience depressive symptoms than those who believe that they are developing at the same rate as their peers. Early-onset breast growth is linked to an increased incidence of depression symptoms, according to a 2016 study.

Understanding Happiness as a Constant State

Happiness is so emphasized in our culture that some parents believe that it is their responsibility to make their children happy all the time. When a teen is depressed, his parents try to make him feel better. When he is mad, they calm him down. Children grow up believing that if they are not happy all the time, something is wrong. This causes a lot of internal conflict. They do not realize that it is natural and healthy to sometimes experience sadness, guilt, frustration, disappointment, and anger.

Shying Away from Emotional Skills

We place a high value on academic preparation while putting little emphasis on teaching children the emotional skills they need to succeed. In fact, according to a national survey of first-year college students, 60% of them feel emotionally unprepared for college life. Knowing how to manage their time, deal with stress, and looking after their feelings are important aspects of living a happy life. It is no surprise that teenagers are concerned about everyday problems if they lack good coping skills.

Electronics Become an Unhealthy Escape

Constant access to digital gadgets allows children to escape unpleasant emotions such as boredom, loneliness, or sadness by immersing themselves in games while driving or conversing on social media when sent to their rooms. We are now seeing what occurs when an entire generation has spent their childhoods trying to escape discomfort. They did not obtain the coping skills to deal with everyday obstacles since their electronics substituted the opportunities to develop mental strength.

High Expectations and Peer Pressure

Teenagers are under too much stress at this age and tend to set lofty goals for themselves. Most teenagers aspire to do well in school and attend prestigious universities. Many students participate in after-school activities and work part-time. Volunteering, participating in community activities, having tasks at home, and maintaining an active social life are all things that today's teenagers desire to do. These demands not only cause stress in teenagers, but they also leave little time for decompression, quiet time, or even sleeping. Sleep deprivation exacerbates worry, making sleeping more difficult, creating a vicious cycle.

Peer pressure has two sides, i.e., negative or positive, but it raises stress levels in both cases. For example, being encouraged to shoplift or commit another crime is stressful and has negative peer pressure. If all of your teen's peers are earning good grades, applying to good colleges, and dating the football or cheerleading team captain, it puts a lot of pressure on your teen to conform and keep up.

Social anxiety is another sort of anxiety that peers aggravate. Your adolescent may fear coming to school and having to interact with others. Bullying can create this problem or develop seemingly out of nowhere. Although social anxiety and shyness are not the same things, some people mistakenly believe that they are shy when they actually have social anxiety.

1.3 The Crumbling Teen Anxiety

Do you wonder what goes on inside your teen's head?

This is what a common school day of a teen with anxiety is like for her:

"Knowing what lies ahead, I reluctantly approach the steps of my high school. I do not have any friends, so it is a long lonely day. I always arrive early because I am frightened of being late for class. I could not bear the notion of being late and being looked at by everyone.

The teachers often pass by me because I arrive early. I keep my head down, too, so that we do not have to say "hello" to each other, which could be awkward.

I know what they are thinking.

What is the matter with her?

Why is it that she has no one to talk to?

I walk into my first-period class and listen to the conversations going on around me. Everyone is gushing about how wonderful their weekend was. I keep my head down and try not to draw anyone's attention to myself.

I do the same thing with the teacher, hoping he would not ask me a question. It works some of the time, and some of the time, it does not. When asked a question, I quickly mutter a response, praying the floor would just open up and take me whole.

I frequently have lunch alone or with a group of fellows, I used to know but no longer have much in common with. I am sure they wonder why I am sitting with them since I never say anything. One of them will occasionally ask me a question. I normally keep my gaze fixed on my food and act as if I am not aware of their presence.

Everyone is probably wondering what is wrong with me.

I have attempted to schedule my lessons to avoid public speaking. Unfortunately, it is far-fetched to completely avoid it.

When I have a presentation or a speech to give, I prepare months ahead of time. I cannot concentrate for the entire day if it is in my last-period class. My heart beats so loudly that I am sure everyone can hear it when I finally go up to speak. My hands and voice both tremble. I have a hard time catching my breath. I am sure everyone thinks I am crazy or that something is seriously wrong with me.

I do not participate in many things outside of school. I do not have a part-time job like the rest of the kids because I am too scared to apply or go for an interview. I spend most of my weekends reading or completing homework at home.

I have not told anyone about how I feel because I am too embarrassed and afraid they will think that I am making a big deal out of nothing.

I should be able to do these things, right? It is just one of the personality flaws that I have a problem in social situations. If I persist hard enough, I should be able to become more outgoing and capable.

My music teacher did attempt to chat with me about my nervousness at one point. She noticed how agitated I became and inquired as to what was wrong, but I dismissed her question.

I was too embarrassed to express how I felt as if she would think I was stupid. Ironically, I cannot talk to anyone about my fear of people because I am terrified of people.

I get pretty down about how things are sometimes, and I believe I am even depressed at times. It is exhausting to be plagued with anxiety all the time.

Maybe once I graduate from high school, things will be a lot easier.

Hopefully, I will be able to start over somewhere where no one knows me and work through my worries. Maybe one day I will develop the confidence to seek the help that I probably need."

I thought I would give you a detailed insight into what your child probably feels in his usual day before giving you a theoretical list about it, but hey, that is important too for your understanding. I hope these effects and signs help you cater to your teen's anxiety. Let's begin.

Sleep Disturbances

Every night, a teenager should get between eight to ten hours of sleep.

However, there are many reasons why a teen could not get enough sleep. This includes using devices because blue light has an effect on melatonin secretion. The problem could be related to anxiousness in some circumstances.

Not only may anxiety cause sleep deprivation, but it can also be the other way around. So, it has the potential to become a vicious cycle.

Keep a tight eye on your teen's sleeping patterns. Look for the following red flags:

- Going to bed late at night

- Getting up late in the morning

- Drowsiness during the day

Remove any electronic gadgets from the room at least half an hour before bedtime. Observe your child's behavior to see whether it improves.

Social Withdrawal

Teens who suffer from anxiety, especially social anxiety disorder, may isolate themselves. They do it to avoid the stress of social interaction.

Anxiety is typically exacerbated by social seclusion. When a person is isolated, he gets more internalized. As a result, they get preoccupied with unpleasant thoughts. Anxiety can make it hard for a person to perceive the world through the eyes of others. As a result, anxiety sufferers may find it challenging to form new sympathetic relationships.

Check to see if your child's social behaviors have changed significantly. The following are some examples of specific behavior to keep an eye out for:

- Friendship interactions are fewer.

- Not participating in extracurricular activities

- Having to spend more time alone than usual

Compromised Self Esteem

Low self-esteem can be a problem for teenagers with a general anxiety disorder or social anxiety. However, low self-esteem can lead to other problems, such as adolescent depression. Your teen may continuously doubt their abilities or knowledge if they have poor self-esteem. He might also go to great lengths to gain acceptance from others.

Keep an eye on how your adolescent sees himself. He has low self-esteem if he puts himself down or reacts badly to criticism. This may indicate an anxiety disorder.

Declining School Performance

Check your child's report cards and progress reports carefully. Low grades might also suggest an anxiety problem. This is especially true if your child's grades have just started to decline.

A worried adolescent may procrastinate and miss tasks frequently. They may eventually start skipping classes or maybe avoid going to school altogether. Anxious students frequently have trouble focusing their attention. As a result, they might not be able to achieve their academic goals.

Keep in mind, however, that many anxious teenagers do well in school. Their academic achievement frequently matches that of non-anxious teenagers. However, they often take longer to finish jobs.

Anxiety and Panic Attacks

The symptom of panic disorder, which is a form of anxiety disorder, is a panic attack. This disorder is not the same as an anxiety attack, contrary to popular belief. Anxiety attacks typically develop over time as a result of stressful circumstances. Panic attacks, on the other hand, happen unexpectedly and are frequently accompanied by a dread of death. However, many of the symptoms of panic attacks and anxiety attacks are similar. Here are a few of the more common ones to be aware of:

- Sweating

- Chest discomfort or pain

- Dry mouth

- Accelerated heart rate

- Throat tightness

- Issues with breathing

- Fear

- Numbness or tingling

- Nausea

- Dizziness

Take your teen to a specialist if you see signs of a panic or anxiety episode.

Unhealthy Eating Habits

Anxiety disorders frequently coexist with eating issues. In fact, two-thirds of persons with eating disorders experience anxiety at some point in their lives.

Anxiety is caused by stress, but it also has an impact on eating habits. People who are under a lot of stress seek foods that are heavy in sugar and fat. As a result, overeating is a possibility. Females are more prone than males to consume food as a stress coping method, according to research. Males, however, are more likely to use drugs and alcohol. Undereating is a way for some people to cope with stress. This is a more prevalent reaction among children than among adults.

If your teen has had a significant change in weight, it could be an indication of anxiety.

Mood Swings

It is natural for your teen's emotions to fluctuate as he reacts to various situations. If his feelings change in the flash of an eye, though, it could imply mood swings. Mood swings can sometimes be an indicator of worry. Anxiety is influenced by both neurotransmitters and hormones. Mood swings can be caused by an imbalance in these chemicals. Your teen's mood swings will be worse if the imbalance is severe.

Finding out if your teen suffers from anxiety is merely the first step. From here, you must act before it is too late.

Chapter 2: Am I Parenting my Anxious Teen the Right Way?

Family environments can sometimes result in more than just suffering. Parents can negatively affect their children's mental health. Some parents place their children in stressful situations, causing them to feel humiliated, anxious, or powerless. These are difficult experiences that we carry with us into adulthood. Trauma caused by a lack of attachment, abuse, physical or psychological violence, or anything else that interferes with a child's optimal psycho-emotional development can have repercussions. Trauma can alter brain development. This can lead to psychological problems, which can then impact how these people raise their own children, creating a vicious cycle.

According to research, family dynamics and environment are the primary causes of emotional and behavioral problems in children. A recent study by the Journal of Family Psychology claimed that a simple spanking on the butt could have negative consequences. The Centers for Disease Control and Prevention or CDC put forward statistics that adverse childhood experiences cause 21 million episodes of depression in the U.S. alone.

Any aggressive gesture, word, or behavior, whether implicit or explicit, will leave its imprint. It will alter the child's behavior and even leave an imprint on their minds. Consequently, children who grow up in these environments or with specific harmful parenting strategies, i.e., hitting, spanking, aggressive communication, or authoritarian caregivers, are more likely to have low self-confidence and develop an acceptance to abuse and have trouble expressing themselves.

You, as a parent, have a significant impact on your child's mental health. So, what you say and do and the environment you establish at home can encourage good mental health in your children, keeping away anxiety, stress, and depression.

Time for a quick story.

John Green, the best-selling author who has given us the amazing "The Fault in Our Stars," explains that he constantly replays the same concerns and anxieties in his mind. He could not even go through a menu or even keep up with the plot of a television show at one time, let alone write a book.

Mr. Green has fought with obsessive-compulsive disorder and severe anxiety for as long as he can remember. He manages it with counseling and medication, but it still dominates him now and then.

In an interview, Mr. Green expressed that he could not break free from the spiral of his thoughts, and he felt like they were coming from outside his head. He added that he wanted to talk about it without feeling embarrassed or ashamed because he believed it was vital for people to hear from adults who lived worthwhile lives and managed chronic mental sicknesses as part of those worthwhile lives.

If you are a parent or a teen reading this, what I want you to take from this story is that even the most influential people with the most meaningful and fulfilling lives fight with anxiety. You are not alone in this, you can have a fulfilling life, and it can get better for you too.

Now let's discuss the right parenting strategies to help your children be anxiety-free and how you can unknowingly be making it worse. Teens can look into the following advice and pass it on to their parents and even look out for the mentioned issues themselves as the root cause.

2.1 Oxygen to Anxiety

If you have an anxious child, you have probably tried everything you can think of to make a difference. Generally speaking, there are no wrong or right ways to parent an anxious child, but certain things will work well right away, some that will be useful in the short term but hurtful in the long run, and some that will be a massive disaster right away. The only thing these strategies have in common is that they are all likely to stem from a place of great love (sometimes tinged with desperation, which is reasonable), but they are always motivated by love.

You will always be the authority on your child, so trust your instincts about what works best. Here are some parental methods to consider that may appear to work well in the short term but are actually maintaining your child's anxiety ballooned up and well-fed:

- **Anxious Parents**

    Growing up with an anxious parent is tremendously challenging for a youngster. Anxiety is a constrictive condition that prevents people from enjoying free and worthwhile lives, and it frequently emphasizes "worst-case scenario" mindset. Add in the fact that many nervous parents do not recognize themselves as anxious and believe their behavior and ideas are grounded in reality. The mother who repeatedly urges her daughter that all men are predators and are not to be trusted may have been raped as a teenager. The father who argues that people of another race are not to be trusted and made friends may be a first-generation immigrant who people of this ethnicity violated in any way.

In another scenario, anxious parents may believe that their anxiety is a good thing. Thereby they desensitize their children to its negative consequences. They may see their fear of the worst-case situation as foresight or even perfectionism as a driving force that keeps their life on track and contributes to their academic or professional success. Some hoarding or Obsessive Compulsive Disorder parents reject their approach and mindset totally, which can terribly affect children's mental health.

- **Unhealthy Expectations**

Approximately for the last ten years, the Leadership Society of Arizona has worked with over 2,000 teenagers and 1,500 college students. The most common concern among their students is living up to adult expectations.

We want the best for our children as parents and teachers. We want them to have a happy and prosperous life. We push them to achieve greatness. However, to encourage children to achieve greatness, we frequently exaggerate their abilities.

Today's teenagers are expected to achieve good grades, attend a good college, and get a well-paying job. We teach kids to treat school like a job, but it is actually more demanding. Students must sit quietly for 6 hours, listen, take notes, memorize, organize, and exercise self-control in school. Most individuals are incapable of dealing with all this in a two-hour office meeting.

On top of that, we expect our teenagers to take care of themselves. This means maintaining a healthy, active, and positive lifestyle for some. This entails financially maintaining their family and caring for their home for the less fortunate.

As adults, this may not appear to be a busy schedule, but for teenagers, it is.

We want our teens to be better than we were, yet we overlook the importance of allowing them to be themselves.

This is why school causes anxiety in teenagers: they are afraid of failing.

This is why they obsess over technology: they are looking for an escape.

This is why they experience social pressure: they cannot stop comparing themselves to others.

Children are subjected to so many expectations, standards, and roles that I could write an entire book about it. Let's have a few examples:

➤ **I wish my child to be like me.**

In this case, the caregiver is attempting to mold their child into themselves. They want the child to share their interests, hobbies, mannerisms, beliefs, and even appearance. They essentially want their child to be a little replica of themselves or an extension of themselves.

➤ **I want my child to grow up to be X.**

This is a continuation of the preceding concept, but it pertains to a specific role, such as a profession. A child is frequently pressured to follow in their parent's footsteps. A parent who is a doctor, for example, expects their child to follow in their footsteps and is dissatisfied or even angry if the youngster declines.

- **Focusing on Weaknesses**

We all want to help our children with their difficulties. We hire a tutor after one bad math grade. We get them a book about coping with bullies after one incident of being bullied. However, we are unintentionally teaching kids to focus on the negative. Most of us gain confidence by playing to our strengths rather than adjusting for our flaws. Those who are truly content with our lives have learned to focus on what we are good at while ignoring the rest. The things we are really poor at are probably delegated or outsourced. Although children cannot always avoid their weak points, concentrating on their strengths helps them develop self-efficacy and confidence. If you are tempted to spend the weekend looking for math tutors because your child is struggling in arithmetic, instead spend the weekend doing things he enjoys. His self-assurance and skill will resurface. It may carry over to his next math lesson.

- **Caring Too Much**

    You feel bad for your child when she comes home from school with stories about mean girls, aggressive boys, and insensitive teachers, and you often express it, but you should not. Our children feed off our emotions and become more distressed when we are. When my daughter expresses her concerns to me, only for me to get concerned, it exacerbates the situation. She expects me to be strong, but instead, I send the message that anxiousness is the 'correct' response to her challenges. We must keep our own concerns in check while sympathizing with theirs, no matter how difficult it is. We must be the emotional rock: the person who understands, supports, and (if requested) advises them without ever revealing that their difficulties give us anxiety too.

    Supporting avoidance, organizing the environment to make it feel safer, or modifying plans to fit the child's anxiety are all examples of protective behavior. This is sometimes exactly what is required, but when it occurs too frequently and unnecessarily, it might obstruct children's ability to develop their own courage, strength, and resilience. It can also prevent kids from learning that the world, while strange at times, is not always as frightening as it appears.

- **Unhealthy Criticism**

  According to new research, parents who chastise their children harshly may be saddling them with anxiety that lasts a lifetime. Researchers collected childhood memories from over 4,000 persons of various ages and connected them with the participants' self-reported mental health in a survey released last November. According to the findings, children raised by authoritarian parents have a tougher time adapting to adversity later in life. According to another study, children who are subjected to harsh criticism learn to absorb parental input to the point where Error-Related Negativity or ERN, the brain's pattern of keeping us on track, so we do not make any more careless mistakes, instead becomes a source of anxiety.

These were the don'ts of parenting an anxious child. What are the dos?

2.2 Handling Anxiety

Here's your anxiety tool kit whenever you feel your child's anxiety is taking over him and he needs your help to feel better:

- **Lookout for Physical Symptoms**

Adults must pay close attention to a child's behavior and search for the telltale signs of anxiety in children to grasp the situation.

Anna recalls her 13-year-old son getting into problems at school.

"He had just returned home and complained that his stomach hurt. He was very ill," Anna expresses herself. "He did tell me he was worried about school, and he told me specifically it was a teacher that he was worried about," she recalls when she followed up with him to attempt to figure out what was causing his stomachache.

Stomachaches, headaches, and vomiting are all signs of anxiety. Teens can have a fast heartbeat or get clammy and start crying. There might be a lot of spinning in the head. They might freeze, numb down, or become highly agitated. They may pace or run away.

- **Validate Your Child's Fears**

I know many parents who say that they do not know what to do when their kids are afraid of things they should not be afraid of - especially if the fear is interfering with their daily routines, such as sleep or homework.

"She walked down the stairs. It was 2 a.m. then. She also woke me up," Amber was referring to her 14-year-old kid. "She did not want to go to college. She wanted to stay home. It was 2 a.m. then. That was when I had to be really careful with my words and not say things like, 'That is stupid'."

Amber's filtered reaction was right. Never reject a child's concerns, regardless of how unreasonable they may appear. A parent's top priority should be their children, "Not saying, 'Oh, you know, buck up,' but acknowledging your child's feelings.

Lewis from the National Institute of Mental Health suggests saying for moments like these, "I understand you are in a bad mood right now. I understand that these are frightening emotions."

It is critical that youngsters feel respected and heard. Even if you are confident that aliens will not take over the world tomorrow, you should acknowledge and appreciate his or her worry if your child is concerned.

- **Help Face Fears**

Validating feelings is not the same as accepting them. So, if a child is afraid of going to the doctor, listen to her and be sympathetic, but also motivate her to believe that she can overcome her fears. You must respect the child's fear, but this does not imply that you should succumb to it. The more you avoid or refuse to do particular things, the child is almost implicitly taught that there is a reason to be concerned or fearful if we don't do the unpleasant things. It is giving the word, 'Oh well, there could be a harmful component to this.'

"It is essential," Lewis argues, "that youngsters understand that life is going to be challenging." Things can be frightening. We are capable of completing them.

But be mindful; you will need to push them a little. There's a narrow line. You cannot push them too hard, or they will break.

- **Building Confidence**

Help them make progress in baby steps and appreciate it. Lewis recalls working with an 8-year-old who was afraid to puke.

"We did a lot of practice," she said, "including ordering vomit spray and vomit-flavored jelly beans from Amazon. We used YouTube to listen to a variety of amusing vomit sounds. We did a lot of practice till we got to the stage where we made fake vomit and pretended to vomit in the toilet."

And, according to Lewis, the girl made significant improvements one baby step at a time. One day she told her, "someone vomited in my class, and I ran to the corner of the classroom," as if to say, "I did not leave the classroom!" She was really pleased with her progress. Previously, she would have bolted from the classroom to the counselor's office, then skipped school for the following week or so.

Lewis suggests that parents utilize rewards to recognize their children's accomplishments - consider little but meaningful rewards like letting your child choose dinner or the movie for family movie night.

These are some general parental guidelines for you to keep in mind. Now let's get into the different faces of anxiety and tackle them.

Chapter 3: When my Teen is a Constant Worrier

Worries and doubts are all part of the human experiences. It is natural for a teenager to be concerned about good grades, body image, family conflicts, and more. However, "natural" worry becomes excessive when it is unmanageable and continuous. You are constantly worried about "what ifs" and worst-case scenarios, and it is interfering with your daily life since you cannot get anxious thoughts out of your head.

Worrying constantly, thinking negatively, and expecting the worst can have a bad impact on your emotional and physical health. It can deplete your emotional strength, make you jittery and restless. Headaches cause insomnia, muscle strain, and stomach issues, and make it difficult to concentrate at work or school. You may vent your frustrations on those closest to you, try to divert yourself by zoning out in front of a screen, or self-medicate with drugs or alcohol. Chronic worrying is also a symptom of Generalized Anxiety Disorder (GAD), a prevalent anxiety disorder characterized by tension, uneasiness, and a general sense of unease that permeates your entire life.

This is the account of a young boy dealing with GAD:

"I had already undergone five years of suffering alone with a generalized anxiety disorder by the time I was 18 years old. With the growing weight of fear pressing painfully on my chest as I entered my teenage years, my ability to speak up dwindled like a smoldering spark. Like a python capturing its victim, the grasp tightened with each attempt I made to break away.

I needed to be free of this enslaving grip. My invisible perpetrator's problem was that I understood very little about its weaknesses, and I was persuaded that no one else did either.

It is tough to see any way out of this cage when you are lonely and living within the confines of your head. A black cloud hovers squarely in front of your eyes, casting a pall over any ray of hope.

I began to isolate myself from people who were closest to me. I was afraid of causing harm to others by actions that were beyond my control. I decided to push as many people as possible away from me. It was torturous for me since I could not explain why I was acting in this manner to those who needed to know.

Anxiety makes you feel alienated from the rest of the world. You are enraged and emotionally tired, making day-to-day living very unpleasant to bear.

I know because I have been there; I have been in your shoes.

This dense atmosphere will continue to claw its way into any leftover courage and strength you have reserved in your heart until you decide what is more valuable to you: agony or happiness.

On my 19th birthday, after five years of severe torment, I decided to take this monster head-on. I realized my suffering: I had the strength to bear this amount of anguish every day, from the instant I opened my eyes to the instant I went to bed. What if I could channel that strength and enthusiasm towards my recovery?

The first step was to eliminate anxiety's biggest advantage: its obscurity. I decided to humanize my condition by coining the term "gremlins" to describe the communal experience of worry. Gremlins can be defeated, trained, and handled.

I began to focus on what stirred my anxiety, what made it extremely difficult to control, and when it was at rest when I humanized anxiety, and I learned how to tackle it. The first time I confessed out loud that I was not okay was the scariest moment of my life, but it is the reason I am still here today."

This is how important it is to understand your anxiety and accepting that you need help no matter how hard it may seem. I urge the parents not to shame and blame their children for their feelings. This way, they will just plunge deeper into the worry spiral.

Consider your brain to be a rocky mountain: a single distressing thought might trigger a cascade of related worries. Raise your hand if this scenario seems familiar.

- ➤ I will fail my test if I do not stay up all night studying, and if I fail my test, I will be kicked out of school.

- ➤ According to a missed call from my mother, someone I care about has died.

- ➤ My elbow has a strange freckle. It is cancer. I am going to die.

It means your teen is a pathological worrier. You must think, why does your child not just stop worrying? Let me tell you why it can be so hard to stop worrying?

Worry can keep you awake at night and make you uptight and irritable during the day. Even if you despise being a nervous wreck, it can be extremely tough to stop. The worrisome thoughts of most chronic worriers are fed by their views about worrying, both negative and positive:

> **Negative Beliefs**

You can think that your constant worrying is bad for you, that it will drive you insane or impair your physical health. You might be concerned that you will lose control of your worrying, that it will take over and never stop. However, negative thoughts about worrying, such as distressing about worrying, increase anxiety and prolong worry. Good thoughts about worrying can be just as harmful.

> **Positive Beliefs**

You may believe that worrying prevents unpleasant things from happening, prepares you for the worst, or leads to solutions. Maybe you convince yourself that if you think about a problem long enough, you will figure it out eventually. Maybe you think that worrying is a responsible thing to do, or that it is the only way to make sure you do not forget something. If you believe that your worrying serves a positive function, it is difficult to break the worry habit. You may reclaim control of your troubled mind once you realize that worrying is the problem, not the solution.

What do teens worry about? How it changes their thought pattern? Let's study.

3.1 World of Teen Worry

The teenage years come with rapid mental, physical, and social development and change. During this time, teenagers face various challenging external and internal challenges. Hormonal imbalances, puberty, societal and family demands, work and school pressures, and so on are all things they must deal with. The majority of youngsters believe that they are misunderstood. Their emotions and feelings must be acknowledged and validated by their parents. Parents should reach out to their children struggling with adolescent growth challenges to address their concerns thoughtfully and courteously.

Adolescents nowadays encounter a wide range of issues that are varied but, in many cases, interconnected. As a result, parents must be aware of the challenges that young kids face today and are ready and equipped to help them to the best of their abilities. The following is an expected list of concerning issues that a teenager may be dealing with:

- **Grades**

  Believe it or not, most teenagers, even the cut-up with the C-average, are concerned about their grades. Good grades are a sign of happiness and success, and while teens claim that teacher acceptance is not that desirable, it still counts. At their core, children understand that a good grade or any other form of honorable recognition provides them with the legitimacy they so desperately desire. The longer they are written off as potential achievers, the more difficult it is to get them back on track.

- **Others' Perception**

Teenagers are particularly worried about "choosing" the appropriate identity. They don't want to be seen negatively or labeled with derogatory terms. Unfortunately, many things one may like, such as outstanding grades or playing the viola in the school symphony, can be associated with being a dork. They may also seek praise from their peers by adopting habits such as smoking or drinking. The higher a teen's self-esteem, the less likely she will confirm her appearance to what she believes her classmates want her to be.

- **Limited Time**

Teenagers are the first generation of "over-programmed" people. That is what you get for enrolling your child in dancing at two years old and karate at four years old. If you did not teach your children about time management when they were younger, you should do it now. Discuss the importance of prioritizing and managing their time with your teen. Perhaps you should do a "reality check" on your own schedule as well.

- **Body Image**

Teenagers can be overwhelmed by puberty because it brings about so many changes. Their bodies change in such a short time. Furthermore, our societal structure promotes an almost unattainable body type as ideal, leading to irrational comparisons and feelings of inferiority. Listening carefully to how the adolescent feels about the physical transitions of puberty can often help. It is also beneficial to discuss social media with kids. Some images create unrealistic ideas in the minds of youngsters, and it is critical to remove these from their heads.

- **The Future**

From getting into college to landing a job, teenagers are acutely aware of the need to carve out a meaningful place for themselves in the world, as well as the competition they will face in doing so. Continue to remind your teen of her strengths and how her attributes (intelligence, sensitivity, patience, sociability) and talents (being good with children, being well-organized, or being a computer whiz) are valuable to the world. Assure your kid that there will be a place for her, even if you do not know what it is or where it is. Encourage your teen to consider a variety of options; the road to the future may not always be clear, but it can still be full of exciting possibilities.

- **Problems in the family**

Most teenagers have mastered the art of appearing unconcerned with their families, yet their careless demeanor does not reflect their true feelings. Your teen is acutely aware of problems at home (whether emotional or financial). As much as possible, take the time to explain and reassure.

We all know that anxiety impacts our emotional state and makes communicating with the outside world tough, but it is also worth noting how it affects what we pay attention to throughout the day. Anxiety changes what we are aware of and, as a result, how we experience reality by distorting our attention. This might have far-reaching implications. The impact of anxiety on attention may affect our views and belief systems in predictable and precise ways.

To use a metaphor from the forward-thinking 19th-century American psychologist William James, our visual attention system acts like a flashlight that searches the environment around us. The finite region of space occupied by our focus of attention at any given time is represented by this "attentional spotlight." What happens inside the spotlight is processed consciously, and what happens outside is not. We can shine our flashlight on whatever section of the environment we choose to investigate in depth by moving our eyes around a visual scene. In reality, in-depth analysis of an object, a string of text, or a place is impossible without first bringing it into the center of attention.

Consider what happens to our attention when we are reading a book on a crowded train. Line by line, our eyes move from left to right across the page, dragging our attention spotlight from word to word. While the word we have focused our attention on appears sharp and clear to our perception, words on the page outside of our attentional spotlight appear hazy and largely unintelligible.

Because taking in all of the visual information from the world at once would overwhelm the brain, similar to a computer, we have a selective spotlight of attention. The spotlight permits your mind to concentrate solely on what matters while disregarding the unimportant. This makes reality more understandable.

While we usually choose what we want to focus our attention on, it is not always under our control, and it does not always regard everything in the surroundings equally. Certain events, such as a strong flash of light or a sudden significant movement in an unexpected location, instantly draw the spotlight's attention to the location where they appear.

It may seem inconvenient to have your attention pulled away from you right away, but this happens for a very good purpose. This involuntary attention shifted immediately to alert us to something in the surroundings that could be life-threatening. In the aim of self-preservation, we can say that visual attention is "biased" toward the threat.

While this function aids in our survival, worry makes this rapid and simple threat detection mechanism hypersensitive, causing the attentional spotlight to behave in a harmful manner. In particular, some control over the spotlight is lost as it is too easily seized by anything that could be viewed as threatening, regardless of whether it is. Negative information occupies one's consciousness when one's attention is solely focused on the threat. Imagine what it is like for a highly anxious individual to travel the train in a congested metropolitan region to grasp how anxiety may transform one's entire experience of the world just by biasing attention.

Consider yourself standing on a crowded train platform, staring into the mob of people waiting behind you. The focus of your attention is immediately drawn to the negative facial expressions, while the favorable ones go unnoticed. As a result, everyone appears to be upset, and things appear to be getting gloomier overall. On the train trip home, after all the stops except yours have passed, a large man in a hoodie sitting close to you reaches into his jacket pocket, grabbing your attention as if looking for a weapon. Fortunately, it was only a cell phone, but it makes you wonder what could have happened if you had not been so fortunate. The entire encounter reinforces your view of the subway as a dangerous environment filled with suspect characters and anxious passengers.

Consider what happens if this type of attentional behavior occurs all of the time. Worry and fear run through the cognitive system as the threat bias filters out the positive and lets in only the negative. As a result, the environment is viewed in an extremely threat-conscious light. Essentially, the world appears to the worried to be a lot scarier, unhappier place. This leads to a negative thinking pattern and pessimistic life approach making your life exhausting and overwhelming.

3.2 No to Pathological Worry

"I was standing in my New York City apartment one night not long ago, phone in hand, continually 'checking.' Checking' to see whether emails had been answered, texts had been read, or if someone anywhere in the world had posted a pretty photo of a plate of food.

Mostly, I was using my hands to scroll through my phone screen incessantly, as if it were a nervous tic—a strategy to help me avoid my worry."

A young woman troubled with an anxiety spiral explains how she copes with her catastrophic thinking, but unhealthy strategies further push her into a dark hole. So let's discuss how we can deal with the problem in an effective manner:

- **Connecting with Sympathy**

  Encourage them to express themselves. Look for ways to communicate with your adolescent. Inquire about their day and what they have been up to. It could be as easy as inviting them to help you with a task, such as cooking dinner, so you can talk about each other's day.

  Remind them that you are always available for them and that you are interested in hearing how they are feeling and thinking. A few encouraging comments can make them feel more comfortable sharing their feelings with you.

  Even if it is uncomfortable, it is critical to acknowledge and comprehend the feelings people are experiencing.

You can answer with "I understand," "that sounds like a terrible circumstance," or "that makes sense" when they open up to you.

It is easy to notice the things your teen does that you do not approve of. However, try to recognize and compliment them on something they are doing well, even if it is as basic as picking up after themselves.

Take the time to show your support for them. Work together to establish new routines and daily goals that are attainable. You might schedule household chores around schoolwork or set a goal, such as doing homework before dinner.

Give your adolescent enough time and space to be on their own. It's a natural aspect of growing up to require more room.

Find a few strategies to encourage and assist your teen in taking time out from schoolwork, housework, or other activities to do something they enjoy. If your teen is frustrated, work with them to come up with some problem-solving ideas. Make an effort not to take command and tell them what to do.

Work collaboratively to resolve conflicts. Listen to your teen's opinions and attempt to resolve conflicts in a calm manner. Keep in mind that everyone experiences stress.

When you are angry, you should not talk about it. Take a step back, take a deep breath, and relax; you can discuss it with your teen later. Power struggles should be avoided in spite of everything. Teens may be fighting to maintain control in the face of an uncertain world and restricted options. Empathize with their urge to exert control in a stressful situation, as tough as it may be in the moment, rather than fighting back or overpowering it.

Be open and honest with your teen: you can tell them if you are stressed out as well. Showing children how you deal with challenging feelings might reassure them that theirs are normal. Take some time to consider how you and your teen can handle a problem when it arises. You can share these reflections with your teen so they can see how you think about things.

- **Challenging Anxious Thoughts**

You have to teach your teen to challenge anxious thoughts. If your teen suffers from persistent anxiety and stress, he may perceive the environment in ways that make it appear more dangerous than it is. For example, he might overestimate the likelihood of things going wrong, leap to worst-case scenarios right away, or approach every nervous thought as if it were true. He can also doubt his own ability to deal with life's challenges, fearing that you will crumble at first sight of adversity. Cognitive distortions are a sort of cognition that includes:

> There is no middle ground in all-or-nothing thinking, which sees things in black-and-white

categories. "I am a complete failure if everything is not perfect."

➢ Neglecting the good while focusing on the downsides. Observing the one item that went wrong rather than all the good things that happened. "I messed up a question on the test." "I'm stupid."

➢ Overgeneralization is based on a single unfavorable event, with the expectation that it will always be true. "I was not hired for the position." "I'm never going to obtain a job."

➢ Preparing for the worst-case situation. "We are in for some turbulence, according to the pilot." "The plane is about to fall down!"

➢ Maintaining a strict list of what you should and should not do and punishing yourself if you breach any of the rules. "I should not have attempted to strike up a conversation with her." "I'm a complete imbecile."

➢ Believing that your feelings are accurate reflections of reality. "I feel like such a knucklehead." "I'm sure everyone is laughing at me."

➢ Making judgments about yourself based on your mistakes and perceived flaws. "I'm a loser; I'm uninteresting; I deserve to be alone."

Teach your teen to challenge their negative ideas by asking the following questions:

➢ What proof do you have that the thought is correct?

> What are the chances that what I am afraid of will actually occur? What are some more plausible possibilities if the chance is low?

> Is there a more optimistic, realistic perspective on the situation?

> What would I tell someone I love who was concerned about this issue?

- **Deep Breathing**

  Practice deep breathing with your teen. When you are anxious, your breathing quickens and becomes shallow, which might make you feel even more anxious. When you take deep breaths, you activate the parasympathetic nervous system, also known as the rest-and-digest system. This calms you down by counteracting your sympathetic nervous system's anxious response.

  Through diaphragmatic breathing, you can consciously activate your parasympathetic nervous system. Breathe deeply by focusing your diaphragm, the main muscle involved in breathing. This can help you escape an anxiety spiral:

  > Place one hand on your chest and the other on your stomach while softly breathing in and out through your nose.

  > The hand resting on your chest should not be moved.

Paced breathing, which you can combine with diaphragmatic breathing, is also suggested. Inhale for three seconds, hold for one, then exhale for around six seconds, making sure your exhale is longer than your inhale. You can also ground yourself by looking at a stopwatch while practicing paced breathing.

- **Exercising or Meditating**

  Motivate your teen to exercise and meditate. Practice with them if they need company. Exercise generates endorphins, which reduce tension and stress, boost energy, and improve your sense of well-being, making it a natural and effective anti-anxiety treatment. Even more importantly, by concentrating on how your body feels while you walk, you can break the cycle of anxieties that are always running through your mind. For example, when you walk, run, or dance, pay attention to the rhythm of your breathing, to the sensation of your feet on the ground, or the feel of the sun or breeze on your skin.

  Meditation works by redirecting your attention from worrying about the future or concentrating on the past to the present moment. You may break the constant cycle of negative thoughts and fears by being totally involved in the present moment. You do not have to sit cross-legged, burn candles or incense, or chant to do this. Simply choose a peaceful, comfortable location and download one of the many free or low-cost smartphone apps that can assist you in meditation.

- **Distinguishing Types of Worries**

Help your child differentiate between solvable and unsolvable worries. According to research, worrying makes you feel less worried for a short time. Running through the problem in your thoughts diverts your attention away from your feelings and gives you the satisfaction and fulfillment that you are accomplishing something. Worrying and problem-solving, on the other hand, are two quite different things.

Problem-solving entails assessing a situation, devising clear strategies to address it, and putting the plan into action. Worrying, on the other hand, almost never results in a solution. You are no more equipped to deal with worst-case scenarios if they actually happen, no matter how many hours you spend thinking about your problems.

> ➢ Start brainstorming if the problem is solvable. Make a list of every potential solution that comes to mind. Do not get too caught up in finding the ideal solution. Concentrate on the things you can change instead of the facts or events that are beyond your control. Make an action plan after you have analyzed your choices. You will feel a lot better once you have made a plan and started working on the problem.

> ➢ Accept the uncertainty if the worry is unsolvable. If you are a pathological worrier, this is where you will find the majority of your nervous thoughts. Worrying is a common technique for us to try to foretell what the future

holds in order to avoid unpleasant surprises and exert influence over the outcome. The issue is that it does not work. It does not make life any more predictable to think about all the things that could go wrong. Focusing on the worst-case situations can prevent you from appreciating the nice things you have now. To quit worrying, address your desire for certainty and quick responses.

Ask your teen to ponder on these questions:

> ➢ What are the realistic chances that something bad will occur?

> ➢ Inquire about your friends and relatives how they deal with uncertainty in different scenarios. Would you be able to do the same?

> ➢ Is it feasible to live with the slight risk that something bad would happen, given the low probability?

> ➢ Pay attention to your emotions. Worrying about uncertainty is a common coping mechanism for people who want to avoid unpleasant emotions. However, by becoming more aware of your emotions, you might begin to embrace them, even if they are unpleasant or illogical.

I hope you have developed a better understanding of your teen's constant worrying. Try the above-mentioned effective strategies for your teen so they can change the worry lens they see the world with.

Chapter 4: When my Teen is Socially Insecure

Ricky Williams is best remembered as the Heisman Trophy-winning running back who had it all: fame, fortune, and talent. Who would believe that after a brilliant career, this football sensation, who played in front of 100,000 fans, hated going to the grocery store or running into a fan on the street?

"I was 23, a billionaire, and I had everything," Williams said, "yet I had never been so unhappy in my life because I could not express how I was feeling to my friends and family, I felt terribly alienated. I could not understand what was wrong with me."

Williams was forced into the spotlight with enormous expectations to perform. He was known for holding interviews with his helmet on and shying away from people. The media often characterized him as aloof or even strange. He could not even connect with his little daughter, let alone leave the house for errands. Most people did not realize that by just talking to a reporter, a fan, a community member, or even his own family, Williams was attempting to address the root of his problem.

Williams eventually discovered that he was one of the more than 15 million people in the United States who suffer from a social anxiety disorder, often known as social phobia. People who suffer from social anxiety disorder are terrified of being scrutinized by others in social or performance circumstances and receiving negative comments. In other words, they are terrified of people. Another fighter of social phobia shares her story:

"I hated family get-togethers and even cried when they sang "Happy Birthday" to me. I couldn't describe it. I only knew I didn't like being the center of attention. And "it" grew with me as I grew. When I was in school, being asked to read my work aloud or answer a question would cause me a nervous breakdown. My body went numb, I blushed madly, and I couldn't talk. At night, I'd spend hours going over my day's interactions, looking for clues that my classmates were aware that something was wrong with me."

More than a third of people with this illness have symptoms for ten years or more before seeking treatment. So let's make sure your teen does not go through the same thing.

4.1 The Alienated Self

When you have social anxiety, it is like having a loud annoying song playing in the background, distracting you from what you should be saying or doing.

What is the cause of social phobia? Rather than a single causative element, the condition is most likely the outcome of a complex interplay of circumstances.

- **Genes**

  If your teen is diagnosed with SAD, he is likely to have particular genes that predispose his condition. He might be 2-6 times more likely to acquire SAD if he has a first-degree relative who suffers from it.

  The "heritability" of social anxiety disorder refers to the hereditary component of the condition. Although heritability rates in research vary greatly, it has been estimated to be approximately 30 to 40%, implying that our genetics account for roughly one-third of the underlying causes of SAD.

- **Behavioral Inhibition**

  Do you know a baby or young child who becomes agitated every time he or she is confronted with a new environment or person? Does the youngster cry, withdraw, or seek the comfort of a parent when confronted with these situations?

Behavioral inhibition is the term for this type of behavior in toddlers and young children. Children who exhibit behavioral restraint while they are toddlers are more likely to have SAD later in life. Because this temperament manifests at such an early age, it is certainly an inborn trait influenced by biological causes.

- **Learned Behavior**

  Psychologists have created hypotheses regarding how children can develop social anxiety as a result of their education.

Direct Conditioning:

These questions are for you teen:

> ➢ Did you forget your lines in the class play because of direct conditioning?

> ➢ Was it common for other kids to make fun of you, or were you constantly teased or bullied?

While it is not a required trigger, experiencing a traumatic incident as a child may impact the development of social anxiety years later.

Observational learning:

Do you know if your teen witnessed someone else in a difficult social circumstance if he did not suffer a traumatic incident himself? For people who are already prone to the condition, this could have the same effect as witnessing it firsthand.

Information Transfer:

Fearful and socially anxious parents unwittingly pass on verbal and nonverbal information about the risks of social situations to their children. If the child's parent is constantly concerned about what other people think of her, he is likely to have developed some of the same anxiety.

- **Environment**

Your child's background can also influence their chances of developing SAD. For example:

  ➤ Your child was not allowed to develop acceptable social skills since he was not exposed to enough social situations as a child.

  ➤ You were either rejecting, domineering, criticizing, or overprotective. Children who do not have a strong bond with their primary caregiver are more vulnerable because they are unable to calm and soothe themselves in stressful situations.

- **Brain Structure and Chemicals**

According to a study, when social phobics spoke in public, blood flow in their brains differed. The research revealed increased blood flow in the amygdala, a limbic system component linked with fear, in persons with social anxiety disorder. Moreover, PET (Positron Emission Tomography), a nuclear machine procedure of those without SAD, revealed more blood flow to the cerebral cortex, which is related to evaluation and thinking. It appears that people with social phobia have a distinct brain response to social circumstances than people who do not have this problem.

If your teen has a social anxiety disorder, some chemicals in his brain called neurotransmitters are likely to be out of balance. Your brain uses neurotransmitters to transfer signals from one cell to another. According to research, people with social anxiety disorder have some of the same neurotransmitter imbalances as people with agoraphobia and panic disorder. Agoraphobia means extreme or unreasonable fear of entering crowded or open spaces, of leaving one's home, or of being in situations where escape is difficult. Panic attacks are irrational feelings of fear and worry that manifest physically as a racing heart, rapid breathing, and perspiration. Some people develop panic disorder, which is a sort of anxiety disorder, as a result of their fear of these attacks.

Thoughts and concerns about what others think become magnified in the mind of someone with social anxiety. Rather than focusing on the good aspects of life, the person starts to focus on the potential for embarrassment. This makes a situation appear worse than it is in reality, making the person avoid it. Social phobia can impair a person's life in the following ways:

- Feeling sad or lonely since your teen lost out on pleasant chances and companionship. Someone with social phobia may not be able to talk with friends in the lunchroom, join an after-school group, make friends or attend get together.

- He may miss out on education. A person with social anxiety may not be able to answer in class, read aloud, or give a presentation. Someone who has social phobia may be too scared to raise a question in class or get help from a teacher.

- They miss out on opportunities to show their talents and learn new skills. Someone suffering from social anxiety may avoid auditioning for the school play, participating in a talent show, trying out for a team, or participating in a service project. People with social phobia are less likely to participate in new activities. It also prevents them from making mistakes that help people learn.

- It will affect how he thinks about himself. According to research, SAD has been linked to increased self-criticism and low self-esteem. People who suffer from SAD have a negative attitude toward themselves. This way of thinking is most likely present in every part of his life. This will probably be his thoughts:

"I look ridiculous,"

"I am going to look stupid."

"Everyone is staring at me."

"I can't get my anxiety under control."

And the list goes on and on.

Negative ideas like this impact how he feels about himself and, as a result, the decisions he makes for himself.

- It will affect how he thinks about others. How does it influence your perceptions of others when you see them in a fearful light? He probably reacts to strangers with fear and alienation rather than seeing them as potential friends.

Regrettably, how you see people might impact how they treat you; strangers will avoid you if you are afraid of them. Friends will gradually distance themselves if you remain guarded with them. If you think of every stranger you meet being judgmental, uninterested, and hostile, your body language will reflect that. People you meet soon become exactly who you imagined them to be, but only to you.

- It will affect how he thinks about the world. SAD patients tend to limit their opportunities. This limitation may be related to home (he may leave home frequently), with friends (he may choose to have few or no friends), at work (he may choose work that allows him to avoid social or performance situations), and so on.

He does so because it makes him feel safer. But how much does this limitation cost? Help your teen realize:

"One day, when you have only a few days left to live, you may wake up and wonder why you did not take more chances. In New York City, a whiteboard was set up for passers-by to write down their worst regret in life. The things that were not done stated, or tried emerged as a recurring motif. You still have time, and you still have a chance."

Let's move towards tackling the problem.

4.2 Coping with Social Anxiety

Imagine you are in a crowded grocery store with your teen, looking for an item that you do not seem to find. It is the end of the day, and you are exhausted. All you want to do now is to get your groceries and come home to prepare dinner. You ask your teen to get a store clerk in order to locate the last item on your shopping list so you can get home. Your teen notices the cashier, who appears to be around their age if not a little older.

The store clerk looks somewhat familiar to your teen as if they went to high school together. Your teen goes completely numb, turns red, and his hands tremble. You do not have time for this — you roll your eyes and say, "Are you serious?" before approaching the store clerk yourself. Your teen takes a shallow breath, lowers his head, and walks away.

Your first reaction to watching your teen freeze-up was to get irritated, and you failed to respond effectively, probably worsening the situation. So let's discuss some healthy strategies when it comes to dealing with your socially insecure teen:

- **Teach Cognitive Reframing**

    Cognitive restructuring is a beneficial technique for detecting and analyzing problematic thinking and challenging and changing automatic thoughts. Cognitive distortion refers to negative thoughts.

    Cognitive distortions are usually dismissed after a few minutes by the average person. However, if your teen has a mental disorder like SAD, he may find it difficult to let go of these beliefs. In these situations, cognitive restructuring can assist him in reducing the frequency and impact of negative thoughts. Cognitive restructuring is based on the premise that you can change your automatic ideas and change your emotions and behaviors. You can ask your teen to practice the following:

    - ➢ The first step is to write down your negative thoughts and the situation that generated them in a journal. Check to see if any trends exist. You may discover that you are fine in professional situations with familiar coworkers but become uncomfortable in social situations such as parties when you don't know anyone. You might be afraid of public speaking, but not of mixing with strangers.

> Next, you have to figure out which elements of your thinking you might be misinterpreting. Black-and-white thinking, or absolute thinking patterns, is a common distortion encountered by people with SAD. "I never know how to interact at social events," for example, overgeneralization, disqualifying the positive, personalization, and labeling.

> Then figure out if your beliefs are correct and what evidence backs them up. Asking yourself the following questions can be beneficial:

Is my assessment of the situation correct?

Are my ideas based on facts or feelings?

What evidence do I have to back up my claim?

Is it possible that I'm misinterpreting the evidence?

Is it possible that I'm underestimating my abilities to deal with this situation?

What could go wrong if my assessment of the scenario is correct?

What steps can I take to make a difference in this situation?

Is it possible that I'm seeing this scenario as black and white when it is actually more complicated?

➢ The last step is to use accurate and positive affirmations to replace each of your initial negative beliefs. In this situation, you may say, "Sometimes I surprise myself, and I know what to say" instead of "I never know what to say at social events."

- **Help Practice Relaxation Techniques**

When teens are nervous or overwhelmed, they must acquire various techniques to help them cope. When they are struggling with acute physical anxiety symptoms, it is very difficult to apply adaptive coping skills. Therefore, the first step is to work on calming the anxious response.

Guided imagery allows your youngster to go on a soothing mental journey during deep breathing. To help your youngster find her core, tell a little story in a calm, even voice.

Anxious children contract their muscles when they are stressed. Thus progressive muscle relaxation is beneficial. Beginning with her hands and arms, teach your youngster to relax her muscles and release tension. Make a fist and squeeze it for five seconds before slowly releasing it. After that, move on to the arms, neck, and shoulders, as well as the feet and legs.

- **Teaching Problem Solving Skills**

Teens who suffer from social anxiety problems are masters at avoidance. They do everything to avoid circumstances that cause them the most anxiety. This may appear to be the easiest way to go, but it might actually exacerbate social anxiety over time.

Develop problem-solving skills in your child to help him or her work through feelings of dread and worry. Suppose a youngster is afraid of public speaking. In that case, she can learn to rehearse in front of a mirror multiple times at home, have someone videotape her and watch it again, look for a friendly face in the audience and make eye contact, and utilize deep breathing to calm anxious sensations. Assist your child in identifying her triggers and brainstorming potential problem-solving ways to address them.

- **Help Avoid Negative Coping Strategies**

The negative emotional and mental states accompanying social anxiety can rise to physiological symptoms that exacerbate anxiety and further isolate a person. One person told me that his social anxiety used to cause him not only "'internal' symptoms like shakiness in my voice and brain fog that prevents me from thinking clearly," but also "physical feelings like an upset stomach, loss of appetite, sweaty hands, and muscle stiffness."

When faced with an unwanted social circumstance, such as a workplace gathering, many people resort to negative coping mechanisms, such as drinking alcohol, taking drugs, or self-harm, to alleviate their social anxiety symptoms. According to a previous study, heavy drinking has been linked to negative moods, heightened anxiety, and other related symptoms, such as altered sleep habits.

According to research, about 20% of people who have social anxiety also have an alcohol use issue. These findings have been found to apply to adults and teenagers with social anxiety in studies.

- **Help Face Fears**

Although it may be tempting to overprotect your teen, it is critical to offer her confidence-building experiences and not to let him avoid circumstances that cause him anxiety. Gradual exposure to new social events will help her develop social skills and increase her self-confidence. This will inevitably require him to push himself beyond his comfort zone, but this should be done cautiously. This can be guided by a therapist, and your engagement as a parent is crucial.

In a 2017 study, 182 young adult smartphone users acknowledged being addicted to technology, and t also demonstrated probable social anxiety markers such as isolation and low self-esteem.

Our smartphones have transformed into a tool that delivers quick and instant satisfaction, which is quite triggering. Furthermore, hiding behind a smartphone will simply serve to avoid dealing with the issue of social anxiety. Although it may seem counterintuitive and even frightening at first, it is far preferable to confront social anxiety head-on by gradually exposing yourself to more difficult social circumstances.

If you have a younger adolescent, make sure she has the opportunity to speak for herself in the circumstances like ordering food in a restaurant or requesting movie tickets. When your teen is confronted with a social scene that he or she fears, be sure to praise and reward them.

- **Teach Assertiveness**

  Many people with social phobia lack assertiveness. By communicating his demands in a calm and relaxed manner while respecting the needs of others, your teen can practice becoming more assertive. This usually takes the shape of "I" comments like "I feel hurt when you do not answer my phone calls." Learning to say no is a vital element of being assertive, and it is a skill that most people with social anxiety lack.

  Nonverbal communication, in addition to what you say, might be passive, assertive, or aggressive. See if you can spot the difference in each of the following passages.

  "Jane remains silent, hoping that everyone will figure out what she wants. She speaks slowly and in a weak voice, and she readily gives up. She has a habit of looking down or away, bad posture, and a drooping head. She fidgets a lot and agrees with everything that is said to her."

  "Julie listens intently to what is being said around her, speaks clearly and calmly, maintains good eye contact, and stands tall. She exhibits care and pursues justice in all circumstances."

"Jack is sarcastic and appears to be an expert. He is driven to succeed at any cost, speaks aggressively, and stares people down. His feet are usually apart, and his hands are on his hips as he stands. He also enjoys pointing his finger and moving quickly."

Your teen's goal should be to imitate Julie's second style, which is characterized by assertive behavior.

- **Emphasize Kindness**

A 2015 research of 115 college students with social anxiety showed that performing little acts of kindness for four weeks reduced the tendency to avoid social situations.

Although the connection between compassion and social anxiety may not be obvious at first, it makes sense when you think about it. Fear of rejection or disapproval is a common source of social anxiety. However, if you have recently done something thoughtful and nice, such as delivering a sick coworker their favorite dish or offering to pick up your neighbor's grocery order, the person you helped is significantly more likely to have favorable thoughts toward you than negative ones.

Earning this acceptance on a regular basis will help reduce your social anxiety, so you may find that talking with others becomes easier with time.

- **Avoid Special Treatment**

Treat your teen the same way you would any other child and maintain the same expectations, though you may need to be more flexible at times. Find activities in which she excels so that she can gain confidence, and have her assist around the house so that she feels like she is contributing to the family.

- **Prepare Your Teen**

  Anxiety robs your teenager's capacity to think clearly and solve problems, regardless of their specific anxieties. If your teen is not confident in their ability to approach a potential employer or answer questions in an interview, for example, their nervousness will only grow once they are in that scenario, reducing their chances of success. Assist them in preparing for the interview, solving problems, and practicing. Determine which areas are the most challenging for them, discuss various outcomes, and role-play tough social circumstances. Teenagers struggle with what to expect or what will be expected of them because their brains are still maturing. Their anxiety reaction can be exacerbated by their dread of the unknown.

- **Model Calm Behavior**

  Our bodies absorb the energy of others around us, and mirroring is a natural component of human connectivity. This is especially true for those in our family who are the most affected by our mood. It is critical that we, as parents, remain calm, as our own tension and annoyance will feed our teen's anxiety. This is what I like to call "owning the vibe in the house." Breathing, relaxation, and mindfulness techniques can all help to calm the nervous system. Once you have become used to it, you can encourage your teen to do the same.

These are some practical strategies our teens can use to escape the prison of social phobia and experience life in true meaning.

Chapter 5: When my Teen is a Perfectionist

I have spent years chatting with parents about their children's unprecedented worry and anxiety. According to prominent studies of college students, over half of them reported feeling "burned out by everything I had to do." Parents frequently close our sessions with a woeful wish: "I only want her to be happy," they say, "but she puts too much burden on herself."

We make this comment as parents with the best of intentions. We want to show our young ones that they do not have to be perfect to be loved. We want to assure them that we will love them no matter what. However, the statement's wording — "on herself" — places the blame for our children's suffering completely on their shoulders rather than on a culture that is fanning the flames of their anxiety. It places the burden of change on children – we seem to be saying, just relax, and everything will be fine! – And absolves the rest of us, even if we may unknowingly exacerbate their distress.

We may be making it worse. According to a recent study, "Perfectionism is Increasing over Time." Young people are under more pressure than ever before from others, including their parents. According to psychologists, unhealthy perfectionism has increased among youngsters, with the greatest growth evident among those who feel driven by others' expectations. According to research, perfectionism is a combination of exceedingly high personal standards ("I have to excel at everything I do") and extreme self-criticism ("If I fall short, I am a complete failure"). Perfectionism in its worst manifestations can lead to eating disorders, high blood pressure, depression, and suicidal thoughts.

Let's explore how perfectionism feels like.

After receiving an A-minus on her first letter grade report card, Hailey Magee, a codependency recovery coach, rushed home from school in fifth grade, distraught and crying. She had learned as a child that being a high achiever gave her acceptance and love from her family and teachers. That A-minus felt like a failure to Magee.

"I was completely shattered," she admitted. "I felt like my self-worth had plummeted far below what it would have been if I would have received an A or an A-plus at the time."

Magee's use of a bad grade to demonstrate her worth is a textbook illustration of a current trend: perfectionist behavior. Paul Hewitt, a clinical psychologist, and professor recalls a bright young college student who came to him, extremely fixated on getting an A+ in one of those ridiculously difficult courses designed to separate people who are not serious about a major. The boy claimed he was having suicidal thoughts by the conclusion of the semester. "I got an A+, but all it did was show me that if I were really smart, I would not have had to work so hard for it," he explained.

Perfectionism is a wide personality trait characterized by a self-critical attitude toward oneself. Setting high standards and striving for excellence are admirable qualities, but perfectionism is unhealthy since it is fueled by a person's belief that they are perpetually faulty. Being perfect is one way they strive to rectify this. Let's dig further into this phenomenon.

5.1 The Perfect Poison

Perfectionism, formerly a problem affecting only a few people, is now a growing cultural epidemic, spurred by modern parenting, social media, and an increasingly competitive economy, according to research. A vicious loop is put in motion by perfectionistic views. To begin with, perfectionists establish unattainable expectations. Second, they fail to achieve these objectives because they are impossible to achieve in the first place. Third, the ongoing pressure to achieve perfection and the inevitability of chronic failure, lower productivity, and effectiveness. Fourth, perfectionists become self-critical and self-blaming as a result of this cycle, resulting in low self-esteem. Anxiety and despair are possible side effects. Perfectionists may now abandon their goals entirely and set new ones, believing that "this time, if I only strive harder, I will achieve." This way of mentality starts the cycle all over again.

Here are some examples of perfectionism:

> Spending 30 minutes composing and editing a two-sentence email.

> It is difficult to feel happy for people who are prosperous.

> Believing that missing two points on an exam is a sign of failure.

> Comparing oneself unfavorably and unrealistically to others' accomplishments or holding oneself to the standards of others' accomplishments.

> Putting more emphasis on the final product than on the learning process.

> Considering it futile to make an effort until perfection can be obtained and skipping class or avoiding a chore is justified.

> Fear of being judged as less than ideal when playing a game or trying a new pastime with friends.

Need for Perfectionism

Toxic perfectionism appears to be especially prevalent among young people. According to current estimates, about 30% of college students suffer from depression symptoms, and perfectionism has been linked to these symptoms. According to scientists, perfectionism in youngsters is thought to be caused by several variables:

- **Academic Pressure**

  Children may be concerned that a poor GPA or poor test results may jeopardize their chances of getting into a good college. Others strive for perfection to receive scholarships. Academic demands can make children feel like they need to be perfect to succeed in life.

- **Desire to Please**

  Some children seek attention and affection by demonstrating their ability to be flawless in every aspect. It could be motivated by a wish to relieve a parent's stress, or it could be the only way a child can gain attention.

- **Biological Factors**

According to research, perfectionism has been linked to some mental conditions, such as obsessive-compulsive disorder and eating disorders. This leads scientists to assume that perfectionism may have a biological component.

- **Low Self-Esteem**

Children who are unhappy with themselves may believe that they are only as good as their achievements. Perfectionists, however, are prone to focusing on their flaws and downplaying their triumphs, preventing them from ever feeling good enough.

- **Success and Failure Sensationalism**

The media frequently depicts people as ideal, from elite sports to the current pop star. At the same time, other news reports make a big deal out of how one mistake turned someone into a total failure. These stories in the media may persuade young people that they must be perfect in everything they do.

- **Parental Influence**

Applause for being the smartest kid in the class or for hitting every landing in gymnastics may lead your child to feel that mistakes are bad. They may believe that they must succeed at all costs.

- **Perfectionist parents:**

  Parents who are perfectionists are more likely to raise perfectionist children. This could be a learned characteristic if a child sees a parent's endeavor for perfection, or it could be an inherited trait.

- **Trauma**

  Children may feel unwanted or that they would not be accepted unless they are flawless as a result of traumatic experiences.

Perfectionism and anxiety have a tangled relationship. The pursuit of perfection becomes a maladaptive way of coping with anxiety's misery, and perfectionism itself fuels anxiety by setting high standards that anxiety may prohibit you from the meeting.

Despite having committed a significant amount of time and energy, perfectionists frequently state, "It is difficult for me to recognize when I need to stop." Then comes fatigue and exhaustion, or a loved one pleading with them to quit. Their 'internal thermometer' for determining when to stop is not calibrated properly. The dangers of being wrong or flawed are frequently exaggerated, leading to maladaptive anxiety. This fear then serves as a signal to work intensely, and people only stop when the signal is drowned out by mental or physical tiredness."

A victim of perfectionism grew up thinking, "To improve my life situation, I not only have to thrive in school but I have to be perfect." She lived in a poverty-stricken home with a mother who suffered from schizophrenia. She strived desperately to accomplish academically to compensate for her perceived weaknesses due to her family's poverty and her mother's mental instability. At the same time, a part of her thought that if she was flawless, her mother would be cured.

She explains how perfectionism develops as a maladaptive coping technique in the face of crippling anxiety. Her articulation of perfectionism promoting a magical thinking about the well-being of others and giving her an illusion of control is perhaps the most interesting aspect of her description. For many, this is the epicenter of perfectionism. Ironically, according to data published in a Harvard Business Review article in December 2018, "Perfectionists are not better or worse performers than non-perfectionists." However, perfectionism falls hard on our teen's mental and physical health:

- **Low Self-Confidence**

  A perfectionist's concept of self is linked to a flawless performance. When a perfectionist fails, they are not only disappointed with how they perform. They are ashamed of who they are as individuals. Perfectionists are afraid that if they make a mistake, others will lose respect for them or think negatively of them. They believe that their self-worth is contingent on their flawless performance.

- **Excessively Critical**

Perfectionists frequently have a harsh internal conversation in which their "inner critic" tells them that despite what they do or how hard they struggle; they are not good enough. When your kid fails to meet their own high expectations, you may notice them overreacting to challenges or feeling an excessive amount of guilt, humiliation, or rage. The inner conversation that a teen has is critical to their self-esteem and resiliency.

- **Being Afraid of Taking Risks**

Fear of failure discourages perfectionists from trying new things. You must learn from your mistakes to be a healthy and successful human and to learn from your shortcomings. You must be comfortable with making mistakes. Perfectionists, on the other hand, are not. They avoid making mistakes by sticking to jobs that are familiar to them or by avoiding problems. Unfortunately, avoiding risks prevents us from being creative, discovering new ideas or hobbies, learning new skills, or forming our own identities.

- **Procrastination**

Many perfectionists have reservations about their capacity to complete assignments. Some of them never begin a task because they are afraid of not accomplishing it perfectly, while others never complete a task because they do not believe their work is "good enough."

- **Poor Health**

According to research, perfectionist inclinations have been linked to mental health disorders such as sadness, anxiety, and stress. Self-harm, social anxiety, eating disorders, obsessive-compulsive disorder, hoarding, sleeplessness, high blood pressure, chronic headaches, and suicide have all been associated with perfectionism.

- **Inability to Learn**

  Making mistakes is an integral aspect of learning and progressing. To attain success, we must make mistakes. Perfectionists can actually make it more difficult for themselves to achieve their lofty goals by avoiding mistakes at all costs. They do not learn the lessons they need to improve their future success.

Perfectionism nourishes anxiety and stress in teens, so let's learn how we can manage it in our teens.

5.2 Escaping Perfectionism

I recently participated in a photo-shoot. The preparations took a long time. We needed to get our hair and makeup done. We bought the outfits and tried them on, even down to the jewelry. I bought a potted succulent for the foreground, flowers, books, and so much more for the background.

I loved the photo proofs, but they were still flawed, in my opinion. In the backdrop, there was a plastic bag and a shadow on a face. Thank goodness for Photoshop!

Or is that the case? Consider the oldest pictures you have. They are probably the black and whites of your grandparents. They are mostly crooked, and the subjects rarely grin. We now have the means to make a photograph appear perfect, and our society makes full use of them to remove any perceived "imperfection." It is no surprise that our children are under increasing pressure to be perfect in every part of life! How can we change the perspective?

- **Teaching to Accept the Uncontrollable**

    Some people hesitate to accept a harsh reality in life. You cannot influence all of the events that occur in your life. They micromanage, refuse to distribute duties, and attempt to alter others. They believe that if they can obtain enough control over other people and the situations they find themselves in, awful things will not happen.

    Others are aware that they cannot prevent unpleasant things from occurring, but they nevertheless worry about them. They are concerned about a variety of issues, ranging from natural calamities to lethal diseases. Their anxieties keep them busy, yet they are wasting their time and energy since worrying is ineffective.

    Concentrating on what we cannot control diverts our attention and energy away from what we can. And therein lies the problem. Focusing on what we cannot change makes us less productive and may lead to the same outcomes we fear. The more energy and time we commit to things we cannot change, the less time and energy we devote to things we can change.

Discipline is required to focus on what we can manage. It is more of a habit instead of being a "one-time, done-for-all" event. Floundering around in a state of hopeless passivity, fretting about all the variables and outcomes beyond our control. Even when we feel vulnerable and uncertain, it needs the discipline to keep pushing ahead step by step.

If your teen is struggling with uncertainty, share the questions below to figure out where you have control, where you do not, and how to focus on what counts.

> Consider an issue in your life that is still unsolved. Make a concise explanation of the facts and why you feel that the situation is still unresolved.

> In this case, what do you have control over? Make a list.

> In this case, what can you not control? Make a list.

> Being completely honest with yourself, on which of the above items are you currently focusing the most of your energy and attention?

> How can you concentrate more on the areas you have greater control over? What would that entail?

We do not worry as much about what we cannot control when we concentrate on what we can.

- **Praising your Teen's Efforts**

  Praise your teen for the effort he or she puts in rather than the outcomes they achieve. Instead of praising your child for achieving a perfect score on a math test, commend them for studying diligently. Praise your teen whenever you witness them being a good friend or treating others with kindness. When the emphasis is on achievement, youth becomes fearful of making mistakes. Consider this: if an adolescent is only complimented when they do something successfully and not when they do not, they will believe that they are only truly valuable when they have achieved a goal or gained the favor of others. Say something to your teen as 'You worked really hard on that.' I admire the work you put in."

- **Taming your Teen's Critical Self**

  Encourage your youngster to practice self-compassion rather than self-criticism. When your teen is berating themselves for making a mistake, ask them how they would treat a buddy in a similar position and what they would say to them. Also, when you make a mistake, model treating yourself with love. For example, "I forgot to go to the bank today before they closed. It is alright. I will go tomorrow," or "I was not paying attention to the stove and burned dinner. I'll find something else to eat for us, and I'll pay more attention to it when I'm preparing it."

Ask questions to your teen. When you hear your kid criticize themselves, ask them questions that will help them see the evidence that contradicts their negative statements and establish a more balanced perspective. Ask, "How do you know you'll never make the soccer squad?" if your teen answers, "I know I'll never make the soccer team." Then, if there is any positive proof that contradicts their claim, remind them of it. Ask them what they are afraid of if their emotions appear out of control. When we give our fears the form of words, we often find that they are ridiculous.

Encourage your teen to keep a notebook.

Suggestion: Have your teen write down something their inner critic is saying to them, then look for evidence objectively, as if they were a lawyer. They should put down everything that proves their inner critic's opinion is accurate in one column and anything that proves the assertion is false in the other. This activity usually gives them a more balanced and objective view of reality.

- **Role Modeling Failures**

Before becoming President of the USA, Abraham Lincoln lost seven elections. History has countless stories of people who failed numerous times before finally succeeding. If your teen adores a certain athlete, businessman, lawyer, singer, or other well-known figures, research their biography so you can explain to them how their idol overcame adversity.

Moreover, create opportunities for your youngster to see you making mistakes in key situations. Then make a conversation about how to get past life's unavoidable failures. Whether it is a professional or relationship issue, we all face setbacks and disappointments, but we often want to protect our children from them. If you think you are putting too much pressure on your youngster to perform, role modeling is especially vital.

- **Helping your Teen Challenge Procrastination**

Perfectionistic youngsters and teenagers frequently procrastinate in order to cope with their fear of making mistakes. Encourage your youngster to undertake the following to help him or her overcome procrastination.

- **Making Realistic Schedules:** Break down major activities into manageable steps to assist your child. Write down the goal or deadline on a chart or calendar and move backward, setting mini targets along the way. Include incentives for completing these steps. Encourage him or her to plan ahead of time how much time he or she will spend on each assignment. Remember that the purpose is to finish the task, not to perfect it!

- **Prioritizing Tasks**

Perfectionists have a hard time determining where to focus their time and effort. Encourage your youngster to prioritize by determining which activities require the most energy and which do not. Teach your child not to overwork themselves.

- **Cultivating Balance**

  Because it is tough to be very good at a lot of things, perfectionists tend to have small lives. The goal should be to put up as little effort as possible in order to do "good enough" work. It means you will have more time to spend with friends, as well as on other interests and hobbies – all of which are vital!

- **Emphasizing High Standards over Perfection**

  Avoiding perfectionism does not mean that your child should prefer low standards for himself. Encourage your child to strive for greatness and set high goals for themselves, but do not place a premium on perfection.

  The majority of successful people hold themselves to extremely high standards. They are happy because the terms "excellence" and "perfectionism" are not interchangeable.

  Enjoying and feeling good about what you are doing and growing confidence are all aspects of excellence. Perfectionism, on the other side, causes you to always find flaws in your work, no matter how good you are. While pursuing excellence can be inspiring, pursuing perfection can be discouraging.

Understand the difference and make it clear to your youngster. When it comes to perfectionism, children take their signals from their parents: if your child believes you expect perfection, they will struggle to be "perfect" in order to get your acceptance.

Even when praising someone, avoid using the adjective "perfect." This can make children feel obligated to achieve unreasonably high levels of achievement. For example, do not focus on the B if your child comes home with a report card with 5 As and one B. Pushing your child to achieve perfection might have a negative impact on his or her self-esteem and performance.

Encourage your child to create goals and standards that he or she can achieve with effort, rather than focusing on the unrealistic perfection ideal.

- **Focus on Healthy Criticism Receiving**

  Constructive criticism provides you with the guidance and insight you need to advance in your job and life. It may require courage to hear, but it is necessary for personal growth and development. It becomes much simpler to receive constructive criticism once you realize this fact. When you are being chastised, you should always think about the source.

  Is the person who is criticizing you trying to hurt or discourage you, or are they criticizing you from a place of positivity?

You can give weight to what is being told to you if you judge that the source is not malicious. Put your emotions aside and put your focus on the objective facts of the situation. You may want to consider whether or not this is constructive criticism.

I believe that it is in the uncomfortable situations that we encounter that we find glory and growth. Receiving constructive criticism can be unsettling and humiliating, but it is essential. Without constructive criticism, how can we improve as speakers, authors, teachers, doctors, politicians, salespeople, or scientists? We do not have any. Appreciate the people in your life who provide you with the knowledge and insight you need to grow. Make sure you help your child understand all this. Remind your teen that criticism does not define their worth.

These strategies will help your teen manage their expectations from themselves and keep anxiety and stress fueled by perfectionism away.

Chapter 6: When my Teen is Fearful Avoidant

We all put off large projects, difficult talks, and intimidating duties as adults because we did not feel prepared. The same is true for youngsters entering a new world filled with unfamiliar and frequently anxiety-inducing experiences. Avoidance behavior is defined as putting things off for a brief period of time in order to get some temporary relief.

Avoidance is a maladaptive coping strategy that allows the mind to avoid unpleasant ideas, feelings, or events. While it may appear that avoiding suffering is beneficial, it actually ends in never addressing the real problem. Indeed, avoidance may set in motion a loop of behavior that exacerbates anxiety and depression, making it much more difficult to address problems, manage, and heal.

Someone who is depressed, for example, may find it difficult to get out of bed in the morning and may avoid everyday duties that appear onerous. They might sleep in till noon, skip breakfast, skip classes, and avoid going to the gym, and so on. They have less energy and less time to take care of tasks when they finally wake up. More negative thoughts and sentiments will most likely emerge from a lack of energy and time. They may then engage in more avoidant behavior, thus perpetuating the depressive cycle.

Someone may avoid triggers such as people, places, and things that elicit negative emotions. Those who suffer from social anxiety, for example, may avoid large groups of people or hang out with their pals. Avoiding these interactions may save children from unpleasant feelings, but it will also hinder them from acquiring good coping skills in the future when faced with difficult social situations.

Some people may engage in "numbing" practices on a regular basis to avoid bad emotions. This could take the shape of drinking, overeating, over-exercising, or anything else that would replace an unpleasant feeling. It is essential to remember that these are merely Band-Aid solutions. They may temporarily block out feelings, but once the numbing habit ceases, the feelings return, and answers continue to elude us.

Teens are already dealing with a lot, both physically and mentally, during this growth stage. They are going through puberty, beginning to establish their own identities independent from their parents, and test driving independence. Adults in their lives frequently expect them to take on greater responsibility, and they are making decisions that will have a considerable impact on their adult lives. No pressure, right? It becomes even more difficult when you add depression or anxiety symptoms to the mix.

Avoidant actions may come naturally to a teen dealing with a storm of emotions and changes. "I can't control anything, so I'll simply stay away." "I don't feel comfortable anywhere, so I'm going to stay at home." Avoidance may feel like the only way for some teenagers to feel "better."

For example, failing an audition on purpose to avoid being in the spotlight. Another example is when a child underperforms in a sport or extracurricular activity in front of others. If your child plays trumpet in the school band, for example, he or she may perform poorly in front of others in order to avoid being in the spotlight. Knowing that they are sabotaging themselves on purpose can lead to feelings of guilt, shame, or low self-esteem.

Let's explore the subject in detail.

6.1 The Suffocating Refuge

Unfortunately, avoidant actions exacerbate many mental health issues, even if they are motivated by despair or worry. A "snowball effect" can occur. When a kid avoids one circumstance, he or she will avoid another, and so on, until the teen effectively shuts down.

We witness the snowball effect in a variety of situations, especially when people are isolated. If teenagers with anxiety or depression have low self-esteem, they may isolate and shun their family and friends. Being alone with your negative thoughts can worsen depression-related feelings of despair and worthlessness, as well as anxiety-related concerns and fears.

Taking care of personal grooming and daily hygiene (also known as "activities of daily living") can feel like an impossible chore for a youngster who is depressed and has poor mood and energy. Consequently, avoiding these activities adds to low self-esteem and the desire to avoid people and activities. Here are some signs of avoidant behavior:

- ➤ Faking physical health issues, such as stomach aches or being unwell that arise abruptly and persistently around specific events.

- ➤ Self-medicating and getting through uncomfortable situations or dull distressing thoughts and feelings. Some people use alcohol and other drugs.

- ➤ Getting out of specific activities by oversleeping or claiming to be too weary.

- ➤ Avoidance is triggered by procrastination or the need for things to be flawless or "just right" before participating in an event.

- ➤ Excessive time spent on phones, social media, video games, and other forms of distraction.

- ➤ Instead of confronting a problem, ruminating, or obsessively pondering over it.

- ➤ To escape painful emotions or activities, tantrums or meltdowns are used.

- ➤ Overestimating one's ability to rely on oneself.

- ➤ Isolating from others.

- ➤ Lack of emotional awareness or emotional detachment.

- ➤ Fear of being needy or clinging.

- ➤ Unwillingness to share personal information with others.

➢ Being more prone to seek out relationships but keep a safe distance from them or ignore them entirely.

For many adolescents, fear of failure is a prevalent characteristic of anxiety. Some teenagers may try to cope with their worries by avoiding school, sports, and other activities that they associate with them. The inability to demonstrate competence or gain confidence can exacerbate sadness and anxiety.

Avoidance can be a reaction to a sense of powerlessness. When teens seek help regarding mental health, they can begin to recognize "snowball scenarios." Then they can identify the "triggers," which are the events that set the ball rolling. Teens can develop coping skills and techniques to manage their discomfort in healthy ways through appropriate mental health care rather than avoiding those triggers. But first, let's discuss the "why" behind avoidance:

- **Social Anxiety Disorder (SAD)**

  As discussed previously, Social Anxiety Disorder is a mental illness marked by a dread of being observed or assessed by others in social circumstances. People suffering from SAD develop avoiding behaviors to avoid any social interaction.

  Here's an account of its victim:

  "Even when I knew the answers, I was always frightened of being called on in school. I did not want anyone to think I was dumb or foolish. My heart would race, and I'd feel dizzy and nauseous. When I first started working, I despised having to meet with my supervisor or speak in a meeting. Because I was terrified of meeting strangers, I was unable to attend my best friend's wedding. I tried to relax by drinking several glasses of wine before any event, and then I began drinking every day to cope with what I had to confront."

- **Low Self Esteem**

Physical punishment and withholding of love and compassion by parents are linked to low self-esteem in children. Children with low self-esteem may be reserved or shy in social situations, making it difficult for them to have fun. Despite having a big circle of friends, they are more prone to succumb to peer pressure and are more sensitive to bullying. They avoid trying new things at school because they are afraid of failing, and they give up easily. During adolescence, self-esteem continues to deteriorate (particularly for girls). Researchers attribute this drop to body image issues and other puberty-related issues. Although males and girls have similar levels of self-esteem in childhood, by adolescence, a gender gap appears, with adolescent boys having higher self-esteem than adolescent girls. Girls with poor self-esteem appear to be more susceptible to ideal body image beliefs. People with low self-esteem prefer staying alone in their homes as they have an inferior image of themselves.

- **Post-Traumatic Stress Disorder (PTSD)**

One of the most evident expressions of PTSD is avoidance. Avoidance is frequently the outcome of a person's attempt to avoid contact with worry, fear, or recollections and thoughts about a terrible experience. This is understandable, given how upsetting these feelings and ideas can be. Because of stories or posts about war or current military events, a combat veteran may quit watching the news or using social media. Assault survivors may go to great lengths to avoid returning to the scene of their attack or visiting areas that remind them of the assault.

- **Generalized Anxiety Disorder (GAD)**

It is natural to worry from time to time, but worrying excessively can be stressful and harmful to your health. It is referred to as Generalized Anxiety Disorder by psychologists. Often, what they are trying to avoid is uncertainty and the unknown. Worrying is the behavior they employ to avoid uncertainty. We cannot run away from uncertainty like we can from a dog or a social scenario since it is not a visible, physical entity or situation. So our brains force us to try to remove doubt by mentally examining the circumstance we are unsure about. This behavior of apprehension emphasizes avoidance of any situation which involves uncertainty.

- **Obsessive-Compulsive Disorder (OCD)**

Obsessive-compulsive disorder is a mental illness characterized by recurrent unpleasant thoughts or feelings as obsessions or a strong need to repeat behavior as compulsions. OCD sufferers may strive to avoid events that may trigger their obsessions in addition to avoiding uncomfortable thoughts. For example, if intrusive thoughts about germs and contamination are a problem, the person with OCD may avoid going someplace where they might have to use a public restroom.

- **Attention-Deficit/Hyperactivity Disorder (ADHD)**

    ADHD is a mental health problem that results in excessive impulsivity and hyperactivity. People with ADHD may struggle with concentrating on a single task or staying in one place for long periods of time. The avoidance cycle is one of the most common symptoms of ADD/ADHD. Poor access to specific brain functions makes it difficult to do tasks that rely on these functions, and this difficulty causes stress when attempting to complete these tasks, leading to avoidance behaviors.

    "I began studying, but before I realized it, I was on Facebook." "I know I should clean out my closets, but I never seem to have enough time." "I fear having to pay my expenses." It makes me so tense that I find a million other things to occupy my time instead." If any of this sounds familiar, your teen is one of the many people with ADHD who deal with avoidance on a regular basis. Sure, everyone avoids doing things they do not want to do. It is, however, a matter of degree resulting in huge consequences.

Moreover, depression is among many other factors contributing to avoidance.

Avoidance coping (or avoidant coping) is considered dysfunctional or unhealthy since it frequently exacerbates stress without assisting us in dealing with the sources of stress. Procrastination, for example, is a coping avoidance mechanism: when we think about what we have to do, we become worried, so we postpone doing it and attempt to avoid thinking about it.

The issue is that we rarely stop thinking about what has to be done. Instead, we fret over it until we complete it. And we do not stress any less than we would if we just attacked the task. We often stress as we consider what needs to be done, then stress as we race to complete it, and occasionally stress because we could not complete it well enough in the time we had set aside. (While it is true that certain people perform best under pressure, this is not the least stressful method to approach most occupations.)

Avoidance behaviors can increase stress in a variety of ways. They are less successful than more proactive techniques that may reduce stress in the future since they do not truly tackle the problem that generates the stress. Avoidance may also contribute to the growth of problems. Because avoidance can be frustrating to others, employing it frequently can lead to conflict in relationships and a reduction in social support. Finally, avoidance strategies can often lead to increased worry.

If you have ever heard the term "What you resist persists," you have already learned why avoidance coping might make you feel more anxious. People who adopt this method to deliberately or unconsciously avoid something that gives them discomfort frequently end up in a condition where they have to confront it more. Even though it seems tough at first, active coping can and should be used to avoid this.

For example, if you are like a lot of individuals, confrontation might be stressful. If you try to avoid conflict (and the anxiety that comes with it) by avoiding conversations that may contain conflict aspects, it will only appear for the time being that you are avoiding conflict and anxiety.

6.2 Fighting Avoidance

Fostering approach is the cure to avoidant coping. We need to guide our children shift their coping to approach-oriented methods. Here are some recommendations for parents on how to shift gears in their approach to coping:

- **Teaching Self-awareness**

  Recognize that self-awareness (knowledge and comprehension of what makes tasks difficult or easy) is a skill that improves with age. Self-awareness can be impacted by cognitive processing issues. Adults can assist children in developing self-awareness by encouraging them to reflect on what went well and what went wrong in a situation, what they enjoy and do not like, and what they are thinking and feeling. Instead of starting these discussions when a youngster is in 'fight or flight' mode, urge the child to take a break for a bit to calm down. Make a note of when you will return to the challenge once your distress has subsided. Take the time to listen to the child, to be there with them, and to validate their viewpoints. Assist young ones in understanding that while there may be sorrow, we may still approach and experience success. We can ensure that the chances of success are high and the needed supports are present. Consider your own difficulties and how you dealt with them in the face of adversity in order to assist children in developing this skill.

- **Teaching Problem Solving Skills**

  Problem-focused coping techniques are actions taken to eliminate or avoid the source of stress. The following tactics are part of a problem-focused coping mechanism:

  ➤ Active problem solving entails taking proactive actions to eliminate or mitigate the stressor's consequences. If the youngster understands how to proceed, the goal is to fix the problem that caused the stress.

  For instance, discuss the situation with the person who is involved in the conflict.

  ➤ The act of planning entails pondering how to deal with a stressor. It includes devising action plans, activities to take, and the most effective solutions to the problem.

For instance, make a study schedule for the upcoming exam.

➤ Asking for aid, guidance, or information from others is referred to as seeking assistance.

For example, request additional practice time from the soccer coach in order to better your game for the forthcoming match.

➤ Putting other competing activities on hold to prevent being distracted when dealing with stress is a form of screening out competing activities.

For instance, to make time for homework, play fewer video games.

- **Helping Write It Out**

Writing about fears teaches children how to express their anxiety. Anxious children have a tendency to internalize their worries for long periods of time. They frequently do not want to burden people with their concerns. Allowing youngsters to express their thoughts for fifteen minutes each day can help them learn to work through their problems. Try to execute one of these exercises every day at the same time (an hour before bedtime is ideal because anxiety tends to rise at night):

➤ Keeping a worry journal allows children to track how their nervous thoughts change over time. Breaking the loop of negative thinking can worsen anxiety by writing down your problems for the day, followed by one optimistic idea.

➢ Ask your teen to draw or write their fears on a piece of paper, read them to you, then tear them up and throw them away for the night. This allows children to express their concerns and let them go.

➢ Make a worry box. This is an excellent tool to utilize before going to sleep. Decorate an old tissue box with your child's favorite items or cover it with stickers. After they have shared their fears with you, assist them in writing them down and placing them in the box one by one. Take the package to your room and offer to keep it for them for the night.

- **Helping Conquer Fears**

Children will face a variety of concerns and anxieties throughout their youth. Teaching children resilience and coping methods for dealing with their worries are strategies they can employ again and over again. Experts in the region offer advice on how to help your children overcome their phobias.

➢ One of the major steps to overcoming a phobia is to help your child name it and learn more about it.

Whether it is a new school, a new activity, or monsters in the closet, I help kids by first recognizing their fear, teaching them an emotional vocabulary to understand what they are feeling, and working with them to recognize bodily sensations that indicate when fear is building and how to quiet those sensations. You can ask your teen these questions to develop a better understanding of their fears:

1. When did the fear begin?

2. What conditions led to its emergence?

3. What is the size of your fear? ("How big does... feel on a scale of 0-10?")

4. Is there anything that makes it worse or better, and how often does it happen?

5. Is there anything the child cannot accomplish due to his or her fear?

➤ It is also critical for parents to notice the triggers that cause their children's worries and to assist them in identifying them.

Whether it is apprehension over failing at a new hobby or a room that is too dark and silent at night, parents should not try to prevent all triggers from occurring but rather allow some bite-sized circumstances that cause anxiety in their child to occur. The experience of being terrified or anxious, doing the dangerous thing, and coming out the other side alright is very empowering for a child. It strengthens our resolve and serves as a reminder for the next time we face a frightening situation."

> ➢ Helping kids speak back' to their anxieties as a method to empower them and lessen the ability of their fears and worries to overcome them is crucial. We can give their fear/worry a name and tell them who is boss by imagining or drawing it as a figure or whatever image makes sense to them. We can do all of these things through play, art, and therapeutically oriented games.

> ➢ Children are continuously observing and absorbing their parents' moods, actions, and reactions. If they expect their children to behave well in the face of concerns and obstacles, parents must set a good example.

- **Practicing Worse-Case Scenario Exercises**

We can practice the "Worst-Case Scenario" exercise using a three-column brainstorm. You can list your worst-case possibilities in the first column. The next column is a list of options for reducing the probability of these events occurring. You can explain how you would recover from each of these circumstances in the third column.

If your youngster is afraid of trying new or difficult tasks, the "Worst-Case Scenario" exercise could be beneficial. Take a piece of paper and brainstorm with your child.

Ask your child questions like:

> ➤ What is the absolute worst thing that may happen if everything goes wrong?

> ➤ Is it likely that this will occur?

> ➤ What is the most likely scenario?

> ➤ Is there anything you can do to keep this from happening?

> ➤ What would you do in the event that the worst-case scenario occurred?

The goal is to assist your youngster in realizing that, for the most part, their fear of failure is unfounded. Your child will also learn that he has the authority and control to prevent unpleasant consequences, giving him a sense of control and power.

These parental strategies can help your teens develop coping skills to manage their avoidance behaviors.

Chapter 7: When my Teen is Sulky and Stressed Out

Forget about carefree youth. According to a new survey, America's teenagers are just as agitated as the adults around them — and often even more so — according to a snapshot of teenage distress.

According to an annual poll released by the American Psychological Association, teens frequently claim that their school-year reported stress is significantly greater than they believe to be healthy and that their average stress levels exceed that of adults.

According to an American survey, stress causes 30 percent of teens to feel unhappy or depressed and 31 percent to feel overwhelmed. Another 36% claimed that stress caused them to be weary, and 23% said they had skipped meals as a result of it.

Moody, fatigued, irritable, distant, and angry are the terms that describe the typical teen. So, how can you tell if your teen is suffering from chronic stress or just going through a phase? Here's how a burnt-out girl describes her experience:

"My feet were burning, and my ears were constantly ringing. But I persisted in forging ahead. I started having heart palpitations, chest pain, sweating, insomnia, and numerous inflammations all over my body. I did not let all of this slow me down - until I had a panic episode. I could not comprehend what was happening.

Accepting that I was truly "in" was extremely difficult. I never imagined something like this could happen to me. I was confident that I would never fall apart because I saw myself as a superhero who could handle anything - my father's death, heartbreak, and loneliness - I thought of myself to be strong and as someone who would never fall apart. And 'falling apart' was synonymous with failure and weakness for me. And that is something I would never let myself be.

It was a badge of honor for me to be able to handle stress. However, I was unable to outrun it. I couldn't do it because my body wouldn't let me. I was repeatedly forced to understand that I couldn't just carry on as normal. The first step toward 'giving in' and 'surrendering' to burncut was listening to and taking my body seriously. Later on, I realized that going through and overcoming this burnout was the best thing that could have happened since it allowed me to be my authentic self."

If chronic stress is also lurking in your teen's life, it might be because his still-developing brain could not fight it.

Stress Sensitive Teen Brain

Teenagers are more worried, stressed, and preoccupied than adults for a variety of reasons. They have to deal with high expectations from their parents, peer pressure, and the continual fear that their smartphones will die and ruin their lives. To make matters worse, the teenage brain is more anxious than the adult brain in general. This could be because the amygdala, a brain structure involved in emotional expression, develops quickly as compared to brain structures involved in decision-making and logic. In addition, a teen's pleasure center is larger than an adult's, making rewards feel more fulfilling. This is especially true of risks made with their peers in unsupervised circumstances. As a result, the teenage brain is a massive contradiction, being both more nervous and more thrill-seeking than its adult counterpart.

This stress sensitivity may, in turn, increase the susceptibility to anxiety.

Stress-Anxiety Link

Clinical anxiety, a medical disease, can be triggered by long durations of stress. Stress hormones such as cortisol and corticotropin affect how the body maintains pressure in the body. These hormones are generated in reaction to a perceived threat and then fade away quickly when normal levels of stress are present. Stress is a necessary and natural response that our bodies have in order to protect us from damage.

When long periods of stress occur, however, cortisol and corticotropin levels in the body rise for prolonged periods, this increase in hormone levels causes clinical anxiety and mood disorders. Let's dig deeper into your stressed-out teen.

7.1 The Beat Teen World

"I did not know what to do as my heart skipped a beat for the first time. I remember being terrified, but I remember being excessively terrified about failing my forthcoming midterms. So, I ignored it and proceeded to class.

In 2019, my medicalized body hit rock bottom in a crowded emergency hospital just over two years after. When I woke up, I was surrounded by nurses, and an emergency room doctor was giving me chest compressions. I had been unresponsive for three and a half minutes, according to the report.

When I was able, I gently told my friends and family that my stress had grown so severe that it had manifested in a psychosomatic cardiac ailment that was now being affected by a mix of mental and physical management. My health's future depended on my capacity to manage stress, but I had just spent two years allowing it to build up to the point where it was threatening my life."

Now that you know that stress can actually kill us, let's keep it away from our children. Each teen is unique, and various circumstances can bring on stress. According to the Stress in America Survey findings, there are some prevalent sources of stress among teenagers. Engaging in an honest and open discussion about stress is the greatest approach to understanding how your teen handles stress and where it comes from. Parents must normalize stress and empower their children to use adaptive coping mechanisms. Consider the following stressors for teenagers:

Academic Stress Teens face a lot of school-related stress, from grades to test scores to college applications. Many teenagers are concerned with achieving academic requirements, pleasing their teachers and parents, and keeping up with their peers. Academic stress can also be caused by poor time management skills or a feeling of being overwhelmed by the quantity of work.

- **Family Complications**

  Stress spreads throughout the family, and everything that affects the family can influence the teen. Unrealistic expectations, marital issues, difficult sibling relationships (including sibling bullying), family illness, and financial hardship can all increase teen stress.

- **Social Anxiety**

  Teenagers regard their social lives highly. They spend most of the hours with their peers, so discovering and maintaining their circle can be stressful. Bullying and subtle forms of relational violence are obvious sources of stress for teenagers, but learning to manage healthy conflict and work through love relationships is no simple undertaking for a growing adolescent. Peer pressure is a source of increased stress during adolescence. To placate their peers, youths can engage in conduct outside of their comfort zones to create and keep friendships.

- **Current World Events**

  Parents are concerned about school shootings, acts of terrorism, and natural catastrophes, but kids are also concerned. Teens are frequently exposed to the 24-hour news cycle, and hearing bits and pieces of frightening news, both domestic and international, can make them fear for their own safety and that of their loved ones.

- **Significant Life Alterations**

  Teens, like adults, are stressed by substantial life transitions. Teens may experience stress due to moving, starting a new school, or changes in their family's makeup (including divorce and blended families). Not knowing how to cope with major changes can be overwhelming and confusing for a maturing teen.

- **Traumatic Experiences**

  The parting of a friend or family member, accidents, illness, or being subjected to mental or physical abuse can all have long-term effects on a teen's stress levels. It is also worth noting that around 10% of teenagers experience teen dating violence.

Your nervous system cannot differentiate between emotional and physical dangers. When you are stressed out about a disagreement with a friend, a work deadline, or a stack of bills, your body can react just as if you are in a life-or-death situation. The more your emergency stress mechanism is activated, the easier it is to trigger, making it more difficult to deactivate.

If you are frequently stressed out, as many of us are in today's demanding society, your body may be in a condition of high stress much of the time. And this can result in major health issues. Chronic stress disturbs nearly all of your body's systems. It can weaken your immune system, wreak havoc on your digestive and reproductive systems, raise your risk of heart attack and stroke, and fasten the aging process. It can even cause brain rewiring, making you more susceptible to anxiety, depression, and other mental health issues.

Here's how a woman writes her experience as a burnt-out victim:

"I opened my eyes one evening and found I was laying on a bench outside of a West Village restaurant, where I had just had supper with friends. My final memory was of paying the bill and going outside to get a taxi because I was terribly sick and needed to get home.

The presence of the police and fire departments came as a shock to me. Because I could not move my body, my eyes raced back and forth quickly to assess the situation and my surroundings. A restaurant cloth napkin was placed in my mouth to absorb the blood that coated my face, neck, and chest. My friend Tommy was holding my hand. I had already established that numerous teeth were missing when the ambulance came a few minutes later because I could not move my mouth to speak. My blood pressure was so low that the EMTs couldn't move me on a stretcher until I was stable enough. I was a young, healthy lady who had no idea what had happened to me.

I had passed out at the top of a short flight of stairs, pitching forward and absorbing the full force of the fall on my face."

It is time to discuss some parenting strategies for your overwhelmed teen.

7.2 Shush the Stress

Some of the most effective and beneficial ways for dealing with stress may need some effort or practice. On the other hand, negative coping mechanisms provide near-instant relief, making them appealing. Drinking, self-harm, drug usage, sexual practices, thrill-seeking, and bad eating patterns are just a few of these short cures. They may provide temporary relief, but they can also be hazardous. They can lead to low self-esteem, relationship difficulties, and poor academic performance. And this only adds to the tension, increasing the desire to flee. It is critical to make your teen recognize that he has options, and healthy choices provide you the potential to take control of your life and address problems. Here are some parental strategies for you to follow:

- **Changing your Teen's Perspective**

  Help your child change his or her mentality from "stress hurts" to "stress helps." If youngsters understand that unpleasant conditions will not persist forever, stress can be a catalyst for growth. Instead, these events serve as obstacles to be overcome and lessons to be learned.

Ian Robertson, a cognitive neuroscientist, likens the stress response system to the immune system: Practice becomes more powerful. After a significant stress response, the brain rewires itself to remember and learn from the experience. This is how your brain trains you to deal with similar stressful events in the future.

The brain secretes the chemical noradrenaline in response to stress. When the brain has too much noradrenaline, it cannot function properly.

It's also not good to have too little noradrenaline too. According to Robertson, reasonable levels of stress can actually strengthen brain function, making individuals smarter and happier.

To get started, follow the steps below:

> Adopt the "stress is good" mentality for yourself. Accept that you would not be able to avoid the stress as some stress is useful and that stress can be a learning opportunity. It will be nearly impossible to teach this mindset to your child if you do not have it yourself. (Plus, stress can be "contagious," so lowering your own stress level is essential.) When your child senses your stress, their physiology changes, and they go into stress mode as well.)

> Rather than dismissing your child's tension, try to figure out what is causing it. A child's troubles may appear insignificant to an adult. However, they appear to be enormous to the youngster,

and they are causing true tension or discomfort to the child.

➢ Assist your child in identifying areas of development or lessons that can be learned from their most recent challenge. Request that your youngster recalls any previous stressful circumstances.

  o What did they take away from such encounters?

  o What skills did they employ to deal with these situations?

  o What strengths do they have now?

➢ Talk about the following with your child to help him reframe stress:

  o Stress is an unavoidable element of everyday living.

  o Stress is cyclical.

  o If you learn from stressful events, take action, and seek answers. They can be useful. Give specific instances from your own life.

Your youngster will establish a much healthier connection with stress and find it simpler to manage once it is perceived as an opportunity for growth.

- **Teaching Active Relaxation**

  If you know how to manage your body, you can move from stressed mode to a relaxed state. You can turn on the relaxed nervous system since your body can only use one of the two nervous systems at a time. This is accomplished by acting in the opposite direction of what your body does when it is stressed. Here are two suggestions for your teen:

  > Inhale slowly and deeply. Use the 4–8 breathing technique to help you relax. Lie down on your back with your hands on your tummy; fingers lose. Deep breaths fill the belly first, then the chest, then the mouth; as the belly expands, your hands slowly pull apart. Count to four while taking a big breath. Then, for nearly twice as long, or an eight-count, hold that breath. Slowly exhale to the count of eight, or even longer if possible. After a few breaths, your body will relax, but it will also take your complete attention. Your mind is too preoccupied with breathing to think about your troubles. Do this ten times, and you will feel a lot better. Breathing techniques are also taught in yoga, martial arts, and meditation. When you grow proficient at it, you will be able to do it while sitting in a chair during a test, and no one will notice.

  > Place your body in a comfortable position. When you are nervous, your body lets you know. Your

legs shake and you feel like running but you cannot concentrate and run at the same time. Therefore you are making the test more difficult. Take a few deep breaths, lean back, and tell your body that there is no need to panic. Then use your wisdom to find a way out of the problem.

- **Helping Tackle Problems**

Determine whether a problem is truly evil or merely resembles one. This entails suppressing the thoughts that lead you to see the situation as a disaster. Here are some facts to teach your teen about problem-solving:

> ➤ Many people cope by disregarding issues. This normally does not make them go away; instead, they tend to get worse.

> ➤ It is best to get the task done first when it comes to studying or chores. Many people put off work or studying because it causes stress, preferring instead to do pleasurable things first. The trouble is that they are not truly having fun since they are preoccupied with the work they are neglecting. And, of course, the more they wait, the more concerned they become. The cycle continues indefinitely.

> ➤ People who deal by attempting to solve difficulties are more likely to be emotionally healthy.

> Fights with parents and friends do not go away unless you address the source of your dissatisfaction or unless everyone apologizes and resolves to forgive one another.

Three concepts can assist your teen in managing a lot of problems:

> Break the work down into manageable chunks. Then, rather than staring at the vast mess, work on one small item at a time. The labor becomes less intimidating as you complete each item.

> Make a list of all the things you need to get done. This will make it easier for you to sleep because you will not worry about whether you will be able to complete all of your tasks. As you check off the items you have completed, you will have less to worry about at the end of the day. You will see the same massive quantity of work and realize that you are capable of handling it.

> If you have big projects, a timeline will help.

- **Empowering Your Teen Emotionally**

Teach your teen to take vacations in a flash. Healthy escapes keep the mind and body from resorting to hazardous, short-term remedies. Here's how your teen can do it:

> Utilizing imagination to take stress-relieving getaways.

> Concentrating your thoughts on something other than the issue at hand.

> Choosing hobbies and routines that prevent other thoughts from entering your mind.

Moreover, it is critical to learn to communicate feelings so that they do not fester inside. Stress is invigorating and might help you perform better. Stress can paralyze you if you have too much of it. Discover the advantages of expressing your sentiments and emotions. Help your child understand these concepts.

- **Emphasizing Contribution to the Society**

Giving back to others, the community, and society as a whole pays out in a variety of ways. It is satisfying to help others. Making a difference entails a sense of accomplishment. Giving back makes it easier to seek assistance when you need it since you will see firsthand that people enjoy giving and do not serve out of pity. Giving back to others teaches that you can ask for it and receive it without feeling guilty if you ever need assistance.

I am sure these strategies will help your teen cope with stress and avoid harmful consequences.

Conclusion

Anxiety is a normal human reaction that affects both the mind and the body. It performs an essential survival function: Anxiety is a warning mechanism that goes off whenever a person perceives a threat or danger.

Anxiety manifests itself physically as rapid heartbeat and respiration, tense muscles, sweaty palms, a queasy stomach, and trembling hands or legs when the body and mind react to danger or threat. These feelings are a result of the body's fight-or-flight reaction. They are brought on by a surge of adrenaline and other substances that prepare the body to flee from danger quickly. They might range from minor to severe.

When a person detects a threat, the fight-or-flight reaction is triggered immediately. The thinking section of the brain (the cortex) takes a few seconds longer to absorb the situation and determine whether the danger is real and, if so, how to tackle it. The fight-or-flight response is deactivated, and the nervous system can relax when the cortex gives the all-clear signal. If the mind believes that a threat will remain, anxiety may persist, keeping the person alert. Physical feelings like quick, shallow breathing, a racing pulse, tense muscles, and sweaty palms may persist as well.

Anxiety is something that everyone experiences. It is a natural and crucial feeling, alerting danger or a sudden, dangerous change through stirrings of fear and alarm. However, anxiety can occasionally become an exaggerated and unhealthy response.

According to a study, one-quarter of teenagers around the world will experience an anxiety disorder at some point in their lives. That is three hundred million teenagers.

Anxiety often hums along in the background of a normal teenager's life, given the variety of changes and uncertainties he or she faces. Anxiety can become a chronic, high-pitched state for certain kids, interfering with their ability to attend school and perform to their academic potential. It becomes difficult to participate in extracurricular activities, make and keep friends, and maintain a supportive, flexible connection within the family. Anxiety can sometimes be limited to vague, free-floating feelings of unease. Other times, it manifests itself as panic episodes and phobias.

This book is focused on equipping parents with the understanding and effective strategies to help their teens cope with anxiety and stress. The first two chapters of this book build a general understanding of the subject, and the next five discuss the different faces of anxiety in a teen's life in depth.

The first chapter begins with a description of the concept of anxiety and accounts of teenagers dealing with it in everyday life. Then we study the diverse causes of anxiety as developing brain structure, ineffective parenting style and influence, struggling in a changing body, understanding happiness as a constant state, shying away from emotional skills, electronics as an unhealthy escape, and high expectations and peer pressure. The chapter ends with describing the crippling effects and signs of anxiety on a teenager as sleep disturbances, social withdrawal, compromised self-esteem, declining school performance, anxiety and panic attacks, unhealthy eating habits, and mood swings.

The second chapter includes a basic do and don't guideline on parenting your teens troubled with anxiety. The first part describes what parenting strategies act as oxygen to a teen's anxiety. Anxious parents, unhealthy pressure and expectations, focusing on weaknesses, caring too much and unhealthy criticism are among the discussed strategies. The next part describes handling anxiety as looking out for its physical symptoms, validating your child's fears, helping face the fears, and building confidence.

The third chapter is a guide on your worrier teen. The chapter kicks off by explaining the phycology of worry and causes of worry as grades, others' perception, limited time, body image, family conflicts, and their future. Next, it discusses worry as a cognitive filter to our world, affecting every part of our life. The strategies to tackle the problem involve connecting with sympathy, challenging anxious thoughts, deep breathing, exercising or meditating, and teaching how to distinguish types of worry.

The fourth chapter is a guide on your socially insecure teen. First, we discuss the concept of social anxiety and its causes as genes, behavior inhibition, learned behavior, environment, brain structures, and chemicals. We discuss its effects as missing out on education and opportunities, his perception about himself and the world, and the image he projected in the world of himself. The strategies discussed for parents on the subject are teaching cognitive reframing, helping practice relaxation techniques, teaching problem-solving skills, helping avoid negative coping skills, helping face social fears, teaching assertiveness, emphasizing kindness, avoiding special treatment, and modeling calm behavior.

The fifth chapter is a guide on your perfectionist teen. Firstly, we discuss the concept and psychology of perfectionism. Then the causes of perfectionism have been discussed as academic pressure, desire to please, biological factors, low self-esteem, success and failure, sensationalism, parental influence, and trauma. Before we move on to strategies, we discuss the impact of perfectionism on a teen's life as low self-confidence, excessively critical, afraid of taking risks, procrastination, poor health, and inability to learn. The effective parenting strategies on perfectionism include teaching to accept the uncontrollable situations, praising your teen's efforts, taming your teen's critical self, role modeling failures, helping your teen challenge procrastination, making realistic schedules, emphasizing high standards over perfection, and more.

The sixth chapter is a guide on your avoidant teen. It focuses on the concept, signs, and psychology of avoidance. It discusses Social Anxiety Disorder, low self-esteem, Post-Traumatic Stress Disorder, Generalized Anxiety Disorder, Obsessive-Compulsive Disorder, Attention-Deficit/Hyperactivity Disorder, and depression as its potential causes. Procrastination, anxiety, and stress are discussed as among the many negative effects of avoidance. The chapter ends by including parenting strategies as teaching self-awareness and problem-solving skills, helping write it out, helping conquer fears, and practicing worst-case scenario exercises.

The seventh chapter is a guide on your stressed-out teen. It describes the psychology of stress, teens' sensitivity to it, and its relation with anxiety. Next, we discuss the causes of stress as school pressure, social anxiety, family complications, current world events, significant life changes, and traumatic experiences. Before we get into parenting strategies, we discuss the impact of stress on a teen's body and mind. Stress negatively affects the immune system, digestive system, reproductive system, heart health, and the aging process and makes you more susceptible to mental illnesses. Changing your teen's perspective, teaching active relaxation, helping tackle problems, empowering your teen emotionally, and emphasizing to contribute to society.

I have put together this book with the intention of helping teens and their parents fight anxiety, so they can live their lives to the fullest. All the chapters mentioned above are thoroughly researched and backed up by professional and personal knowledge. Moreover, I have incorporated stories of teens struggling with anxiety throughout the book, so you can relate better to your problems.

If this book lined with my intention to help you as a parent, please leave a comment on Amazon.

www.ingramcontent.com/pod-product-compliance
Lightning Source LLC
Chambersburg PA
CBHW071008120626
46546CB00003B/997